Interactive Notebooks

SCIENCE

Grade 1

Credits

Author: Holly Rafidi
Content Editors: Elise Craver, Christine Schwab, Angela Triplett

Visit *carsondellosa.com* for correlations to Common Core, state, national, and Canadian provincial standards.

Carson-Dellosa Publishing, LLC
PO Box 35665
Greensboro, NC 27425 USA
carsondellosa.com

978-1-4838-3121-3
01-341157784

Table of Contents

© Carson-Dellosa • CD-104905

What Are Interactive Notebooks?

Interactive notebooks are a unique form of note taking. Teachers guide students through creating pages of notes on new topics. Instead of being in the traditional linear, handwritten format, notes are colorful and spread across the pages. Notes also often include drawings, diagrams, and 3-D elements to make the material understandable and relevant. Students are encouraged to complete their notebook pages in ways that make sense to them. With this personalization, no two pages are exactly the same.

Because of their creative nature, interactive notebooks allow students to be active participants in their own learning. Teachers can easily differentiate pages to address the levels and needs of each learner. The notebooks are arranged sequentially, and students can create tables of contents as they create pages, making it simple for students to use their notebooks for reference throughout the year. The interactive, easily personalized format makes interactive notebooks ideal for engaging students in learning new concepts.

Using interactive notebooks can take as much or as little time as you like. Students will initially take longer to create pages but will get faster as they become familiar with the process of creating pages. You may choose to only create a notebook page as a class at the beginning of each unit, or you may choose to create a new page for each topic within a unit. You can decide what works best for your students and schedule.

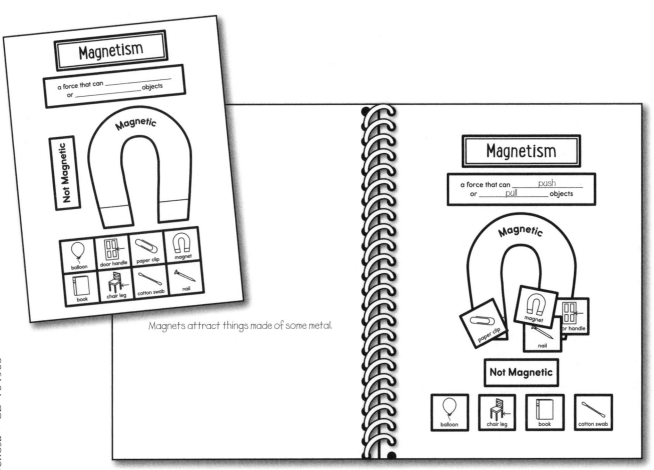

A student's interactive notebook for magnetism

Getting Started

You can start using interactive notebooks at any point in the school year. Use the following guidelines to help you get started in your classroom. (For more specific details, management ideas, and tips, see page 10.)

1. Plan each notebook.

Use the planning template (page 9) to lay out a general plan for the topics you plan to cover in each notebook for the year.

2. Choose a notebook type.

Interactive notebooks are usually either single-subject, spiral-bound notebooks, composition books, or three-ring binders with loose-leaf paper. Each type presents pros and cons. See page 5 for a more in-depth look at each type of notebook.

3. Allow students to personalize their notebooks.

Have students decorate their notebook covers, as well as add their names and subjects. This provides a sense of ownership and emphasizes the personalized nature of the notebooks.

4. Number the pages and create the table of contents.

Have students number the bottom outside corner of each page, front and back. When completing a new page, adding a table of contents entry will be easy. Have students title the first page of each notebook "Table of Contents." Have them leave several blank pages at the front of each notebook for the table of contents. Refer to your general plan for an idea of about how many entries students will be creating.

5. Start creating pages.

Always begin a new page by adding an entry to the table of contents. Create the first notebook pages along with students to model proper format and expectations.

This book contains individual topics for you to introduce. Use the pages in the order that best fits your curriculum. You may also choose to alter the content presented to better match your school's curriculum. The provided lesson plans often do not instruct students to add color. Students should make their own choices about personalizing the content in ways that make sense to them. Encourage students to highlight and color the pages as they desire while creating them.

After introducing topics, you may choose to add more practice pages. Use the reproducibles (pages 78–96) to easily create new notebook pages for practice or to introduce topics not addressed in this book.

Use the grading rubric (page 11) to grade students' interactive notebooks at various points throughout the year. Provide students copies of the rubric to glue into their notebooks and refer to as they create pages.

What Type of Notebook Should I Use?

Spiral Notebook

The pages in this book are formatted for a standard one-subject notebook.

Pros

- Notebook can be folded in half.
- Page size is larger.
- It is inexpensive.
- It often comes with pockets for storing materials.

Cons

- Pages can easily fall out.
- Spirals can snag or become misshapen.
- Page count and size vary widely.
- It is not as durable as a binder.

Tips

- Encase the spiral in duct tape to make it more durable.
- Keep the notebooks in a central place to prevent them from getting damaged in desks.

Composition Notebook

Pros

- Pages don't easily fall out.
- Page size and page count are standard.
- It is inexpensive.

Cons

- Notebook cannot be folded in half.
- Page size is smaller.
- It is not as durable as a binder.

Tips

- Copy pages meant for standard-sized notebooks at 85 or 90 percent. Test to see which works better for your notebook.

Binder with Loose-Leaf Paper

Pros

- Pages can be easily added, moved, or removed.
- Pages can be removed individually for grading.
- You can add full-page printed handouts.
- It has durable covers.

Cons

- Pages can easily fall out.
- Pages aren't durable.
- It is more expensive than a notebook.
- Students can easily misplace or lose pages.
- Larger size makes it more difficult to store.

Tips

- Provide hole reinforcers for damaged pages.

How to Organize an Interactive Notebook

You may organize an interactive notebook in many different ways. You may choose to organize it by unit and work sequentially through the book. Or, you may choose to create different sections that you will revisit and add to throughout the year. Choose the format that works best for your students and subject.

An interactive notebook includes different types of pages in addition to the pages students create. Non-content pages you may want to add include the following:

Title Page

This page is useful for quickly identifying notebooks. It is especially helpful in classrooms that use multiple interactive notebooks for different subjects. Have students write the subject (such as "Science") on the title page of each interactive notebook. They should also include their full names. You may choose to have them include other information such as the teacher's name, classroom number, or class period.

Table of Contents

The table of contents is an integral part of the interactive notebook. It makes referencing previously created pages quick and easy for students. Make sure that students leave several pages at the beginning of each notebook for a table of contents.

Expectations and Grading Rubric

It is helpful for each student to have a copy of the expectations for creating interactive notebook pages. You may choose to include a list of expectations for parents and students to sign, as well as a grading rubric (page 11).

Unit Title Pages

Consider using a single page at the beginning of each section to separate it. Title the page with the unit name. Add a tab (page 78) to the edge of the page to make it easy to flip to the unit. Add a table of contents for only the pages in that unit.

Glossary

Reserve a six-page section at the back of the notebook where students can create a glossary. Draw a line to split in half the front and back of each page, creating 24 sections. Combine Q and R and Y and Z to fit the entire alphabet. Have students add an entry as each new vocabulary word is introduced.

Formatting Student Notebook Pages

The other major consideration for planning an interactive notebook is how to treat the left and right sides of a notebook spread. Interactive journals are usually viewed with the notebook open flat. This creates a left side and a right side. You have several options for how to treat the two sides of the spread.

Traditionally, the right side is used for the teacher-directed part of the lesson, and the left side is used for students to interact with the lesson content. The lessons in this book use this format. However, you may prefer to switch the order for your class so that the teacher-directed learning is on the left and the student input is on the right.

It can also be important to include standards, learning objectives, or essential questions in interactive notebooks. You may choose to write these on the top-left side of each page before completing the teacher-directed page on the right side. You may also choose to have students include the "Introduction" part of each lesson in that same top-left section. This is the *in, through, out* method. Students enter *in* the lesson on the top left of the page, go *through* the lesson on the right page, and exit *out* of the lesson on the bottom left with a reflection activity.

The following chart details different types of items and activities that you could include on each side.

Left Side Student Output	Right Side Teacher-Directed Learning
• learning objectives • essential questions • I Can statements • brainstorming • making connections • summarizing • making conclusions • practice problems • opinions • questions • mnemonics • drawings and diagrams	• vocabulary and definitions • mini-lessons • folding activities • steps in a process • example problems • notes • diagrams • graphic organizers • hints and tips • big ideas

Planning for the Year

Making a general plan for interactive notebooks will help with planning, grading, and testing throughout the year. You do not need to plan every single page, but knowing what topics you will cover and in what order can be helpful in many ways.

Use the Interactive Notebook Plan (page 9) to plan your units and topics and where they should be placed in the notebooks. Remember to include enough pages at the beginning for the non-content pages, such as the title page, table of contents, and grading rubric. You may also want to leave a page at the beginning of each unit to place a mini table of contents for just that section.

In addition, when planning new pages, it can be helpful to sketch the pieces you will need to create. Use the following notebook template and notes to plan new pages.

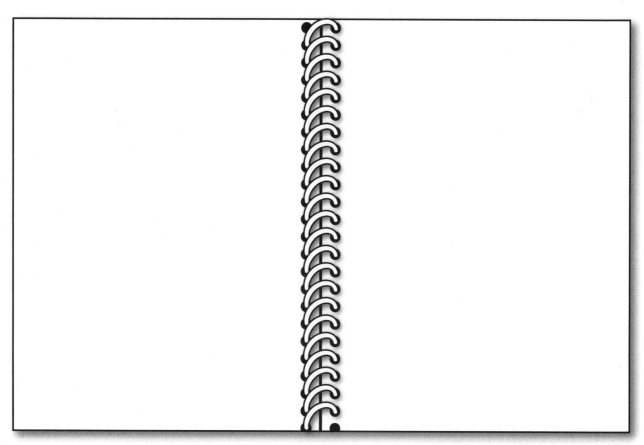

Left Side   **Right Side**

Notes

_____

_____

_____

Interactive Notebook Plan

Page	Topic	Page	Topic
1		51	
2		52	
3		53	
4		54	
5		55	
6		56	
7		57	
8		58	
9		59	
10		60	
11		61	
12		62	
13		63	
14		64	
15		65	
16		66	
17		67	
18		68	
19		69	
20		70	
21		71	
22		72	
23		73	
24		74	
25		75	
26		76	
27		77	
28		78	
29		79	
30		80	
31		81	
32		82	
33		83	
34		84	
35		85	
36		86	
37		87	
38		88	
39		89	
40		90	
41		91	
42		92	
43		93	
44		94	
45		95	
46		96	
47		97	
48		98	
49		99	
50		100	

Managing Interactive Notebooks in the Classroom

Working with Younger Students

- Use your yearly plan to preprogram a table of contents that you can copy and give to students to glue into their notebooks, instead of writing individual entries.

- Have assistants or parent volunteers precut pieces.

- Create glue sponges to make gluing easier. Place large sponges in plastic containers with white glue. The sponges will absorb the glue. Students can wipe the backs of pieces across the sponges to apply the glue with less mess.

Creating Notebook Pages

- For storing loose pieces, add a pocket to the inside back cover. Use the envelope pattern (page 81), an envelope, a jumbo library pocket, or a resealable plastic bag. Or, tape the bottom and side edges of the two last pages of the notebook together to create a large pocket.

- When writing under flaps, have students trace the outline of each flap so that they can visualize the writing boundary.

- Where the dashed line will be hidden on the inside of the fold, have students first fold the piece in the opposite direction so that they can see the dashed line. Then, students should fold the piece back the other way along the same fold line to create the fold in the correct direction.

- To avoid losing pieces, have students keep all of their scraps on their desks until they have finished each page.

- To contain paper scraps and avoid multiple trips to the trash can, provide small groups with small buckets or tubs.

- For students who run out of room, keep full and half sheets available. Students can glue these to the bottom of the pages and fold them up when not in use.

Dealing with Absences

- Create a model notebook for absent students to reference when they return to school.

- Have students cut a second set of pieces as they work on their own pages.

Using the Notebook

- To organize sections of the notebook, provide each student with a sheet of tabs (page 78).

- To easily find the next blank page, either cut off the top-right corner of each page as it is used or attach a long piece of yarn or ribbon to the back cover to be used as a bookmark.

Interactive Notebook Grading Rubric

4

_____ Table of contents is complete.

_____ All notebook pages are included.

_____ All notebook pages are complete.

_____ Notebook pages are neat and organized.

_____ Information is correct.

_____ Pages show personalization, evidence of learning, and original ideas.

3

_____ Table of contents is mostly complete.

_____ One notebook page is missing.

_____ Notebook pages are mostly complete.

_____ Notebook pages are mostly neat and organized.

_____ Information is mostly correct.

_____ Pages show some personalization, evidence of learning, and original ideas.

2

_____ Table of contents is missing a few entries.

_____ A few notebook pages are missing.

_____ A few notebook pages are incomplete.

_____ Notebook pages are somewhat messy and unorganized.

_____ Information has several errors.

_____ Pages show little personalization, evidence of learning, or original ideas.

1

_____ Table of contents is incomplete.

_____ Many notebook pages are missing.

_____ Many notebook pages are incomplete.

_____ Notebook pages are too messy and unorganized to use.

_____ Information is incorrect.

_____ Pages show no personalization, evidence of learning, or original ideas.

Using My Five Senses

Review and discuss the five senses and how we observe our surroundings using these five senses. Have students play a senses version of Simon Says. For example, say "Simon says point to the body part you use to see with," or "Pat the body part you use to smell with." Display examples of objects from around the room and have students use their five senses to observe the objects. Then, divide the class into small groups. Give each group a few objects to observe. Have students discuss the senses they used to observe each object.

Creating the Notebook Page

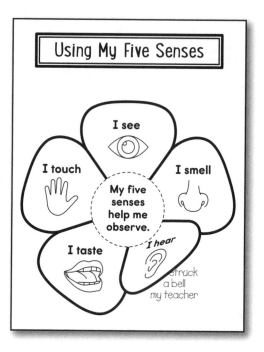

Using My Five Senses

I see

I touch

I smell

My five senses help me observe.

I taste

I hear

struck a bell my teacher

Guide students through the following steps to complete the right-hand page in their notebooks.

1. Add a Table of Contents entry for the Using My Five Senses pages.

2. Cut out the title and glue it to the top of the page.

3. Cut out the flower piece. Cut on the solid lines to create five petal-shaped flaps. Apply glue to the back of the center section and attach it to the page.

4. Under each flap, write words or draw pictures describing objects that you can see, smell, hear, taste, and touch.

Reflect on Learning

To complete the left-hand page, have students use vocabulary clues from the right-hand page to write sentences about each of their five senses. For example, *I use my eyes to see all of the colors of my crayons.*

Using My Five Senses

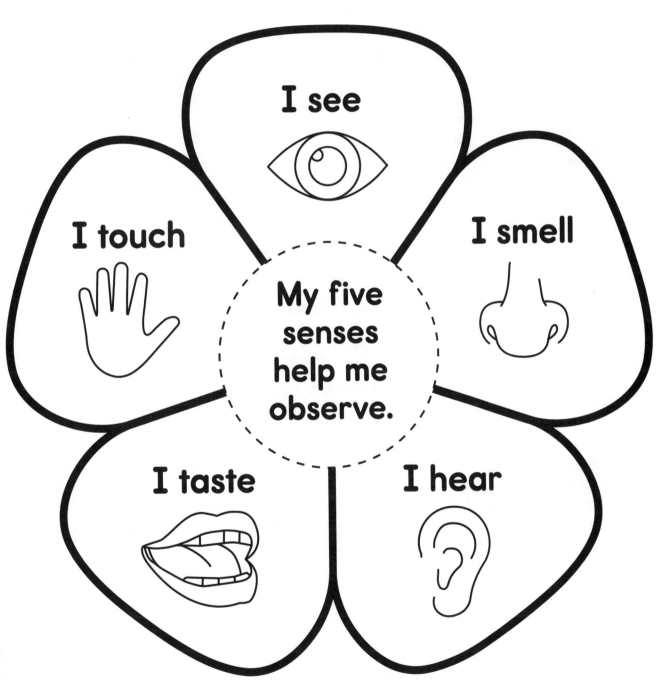

Living and Nonliving Things

Display pictures of a living and a nonliving object. Ask students which picture shows a living thing. Have students discuss the differences between the two pictures. Write their ideas on the board. Remind students that living things have specific characteristics. As a class, list characteristics of living things, such as the ability to grow, move independently, eat, breathe, etc. List students' responses on the board.

Creating the Notebook Page

Guide students through the following steps to complete the right-hand page in their notebooks.

1. Add a Table of Contents entry for the Living and Nonliving Things pages.

2. Cut out the title and glue it to the top of the page.

3. Cut out the flap book. Apply glue to the back of the center section and attach it to the page.

4. Write three characteristics of living and nonliving things on the top of each flap.

5. Cut out the picture cards. Look at each picture. Decide whether the picture represents a living thing or a nonliving thing. Glue each picture under the correct flap.

6. Draw a living object and a nonliving object below the flap book under the correct category.

Reflect on Learning

To complete the left-hand page, have students make a T-chart labeled *Living* and *Nonliving*. Provide students with magazines or newspapers. Have students cut out pictures of living and nonliving objects and glue them into the correct columns.

Living and Nonliving Things

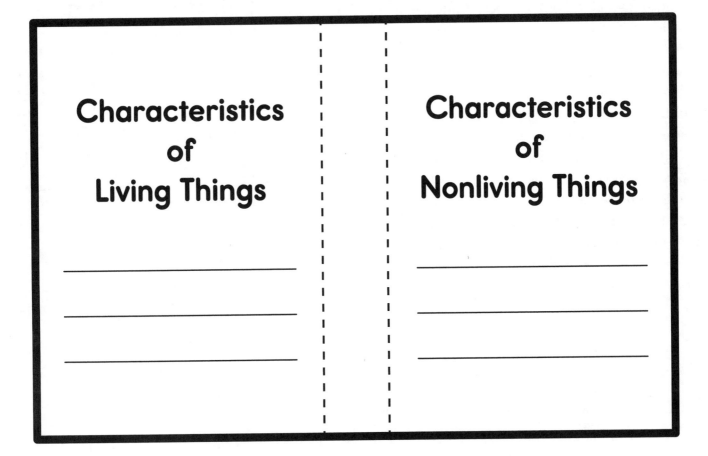

Characteristics of Living Things

_____

_____

_____

Characteristics of Nonliving Things

_____

_____

_____

ball

cat

ice cream

flower

book

rabbit

Healthy Habits

Introduction

Instruct students to jog in place for one minute. Then, have students put their hands over their hearts and feel their heartbeats. Discuss with students the important job of the heart and remind them that exercising is a healthy habit to keep our hearts and bodies strong. Ask students to share other examples of healthy and unhealthy habits. Draw a T-chart on the board labeled *Healthy* and *Unhealthy* and list students' ideas.

Caution: Exercise activities may require adult supervision. Before beginning any exercise activity, ask families' permission. Students should always warm up prior to beginning any exercise activity and should stop immediately if they feel any discomfort during exercise.

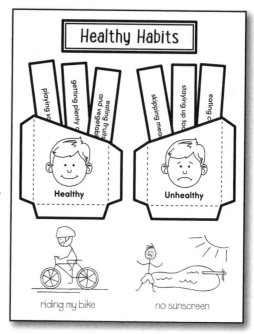

Creating the Notebook Page

Guide students through the following steps to complete the right-hand page in their notebooks.

1. Add a Table of Contents entry for the Healthy Habits pages.

2. Cut out the title and glue it to the top of the page.

3. Cut out the *Healthy* and *Unhealthy* pockets. Apply glue to the back of the tabs and attach them to the center of the page to create two pockets.

4. Cut out the habits pieces. Read each habit and decide whether it is a healthy habit or an unhealthy habit. Place each habit in the correct pocket.

5. Below each pocket, write or draw one more healthy and unhealthy choice.

Reflect on Learning

To complete the left-hand page, provide students with magazines or newspapers. Have students draw lines to divide their pages into two sections labeled *Unhealthy Habits* and *Healthy Habits*. Have students cut out pictures that represent healthy and unhealthy habits and glue the pictures into the correct sections.

Healthy Habits

Healthy

Unhealthy

playing soccer	staying up too late
eating candy	eating fruits and vegetables
getting plenty of rest	skipping meals

Parts of a Plant

Introduction

Display a picture of a plant. Identify and review the basic parts of a plant and their functions. Then, have students stand to demonstrate that their bodies are like the parts of the plant. Explain that their feet are like the roots of the plant and keep the plant firmly in the soil. The stem of the plant holds the plant up, just as students' bodies hold them up. The leaves of the plant extend from the stem just as students' arms extend from their bodies. Finally, the flower of the plant is at the top just as students' heads are at the top of their bodies.

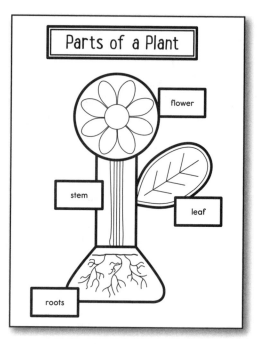

Creating the Notebook Page

Guide students through the following steps to complete the right-hand page in their notebooks.

1. Add a Table of Contents entry for the Parts of a Plant pages.

2. Cut out the title and glue it to the top of the page.

3. Cut out the plant part picture pieces. Place the pieces in the correct order to construct a plant. Glue each piece to the page.

4. Cut out the word cards. Glue the correct word next to the correct plant part to create a diagram.

Reflect on Learning

To complete the left-hand page, write the following sentences on the board: *A plant has _____. The _____ help(s) the plant to _____.* Each student should copy the sentence, choose one of the plant parts, and use the part to complete the sentences.

Parts of a Plant

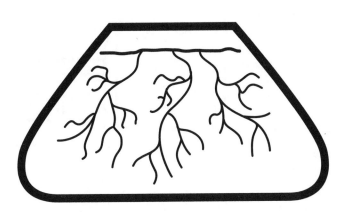

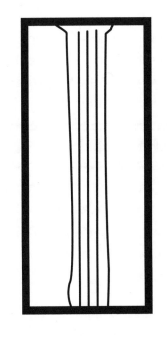

| roots | leaf | stem | flower |

Plants Need and Give

Display a bottle of water, a piece of paper, a piece of fruit, and some soil. Have students explain which items plants need and which items come from plants. Explain that plants need things to grow, but plants give us many things as well. Have students work in two groups. One group should make a list of plant needs and the other group should make a list of things that plants give us. Have students write or draw their ideas on chart paper. Have each group discuss and share their lists.

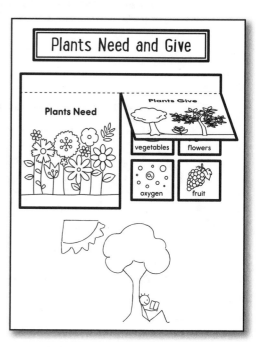

Creating the Notebook Page

Guide students through the following steps to complete the right-hand page in their notebooks.

1. Add a Table of Contents entry for the Plants Need and Give pages.

2. Cut out the title and glue it to the top of the page.

3. Cut out the *Plants Need/Plants Give* flap book. Cut on the solid line to create two flaps. Apply glue to the back of the top section and attach it to the page below the title.

4. Cut out the picture cards. Look at each picture and decide whether it is what a plant needs or what a plant gives to humans and animals. Glue each picture under the correct flap.

5. Below the flap book, draw a picture of yourself using something that a plant gives.

Reflect on Learning

To complete the left-hand page, have students use the picture clues on the right-hand page to write two sentences about plants. For example, *Plants need air and water to grow.* or *Trees give us apples to eat.*

Plants Need and Give

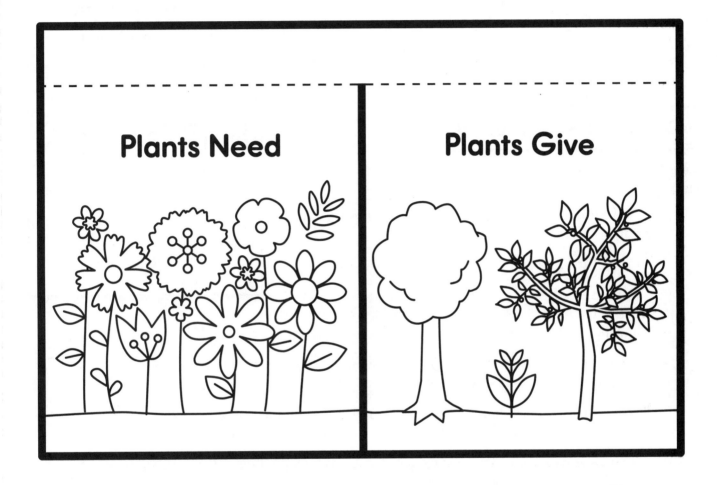

Plants Need

Plants Give

soil

water

fruit

air

oxygen

flowers

vegetables

sunlight

Frog Life Cycle

Introduction

Discuss the concept of a life cycle. Ask students how they think the frog starts its life cycle. Write their ideas on the board. Describe the frog life cycle stages: egg, tadpole, tadpole with legs, froglet, and frog. If available, show a short video or pictures of each stage of a frog's life cycle. Then, have students act out the life cycle of a frog.

Creating the Notebook Page

Guide students through the following steps to complete the right-hand page in their notebooks.

1. Add a Table of Contents entry for the Frog Life Cycle pages.

2. Cut out the title and glue it to the top of the page.

3. Cut out the flap book. Cut on the solid lines to create five flaps. Apply glue to the back of the top section and attach it to the page.

4. Cut out the picture cards. Look at each picture and decide which stage of the frog's life cycle it represents. Glue each picture under the correct flap.

5. Draw an arrow from the *5th* flap to the *1st* flap around the bottom of the flap book to connect the stages and represent how the life cycle begins again.

6. Below the flap book, write a sentence to explain how the frog's life cycle begins again.

Reflect on Learning

To complete the left-hand page, have students draw a pond scene. Students should draw a frog in one of its life stages in or near the pond and label the life cycle stage.

Frog Life Cycle

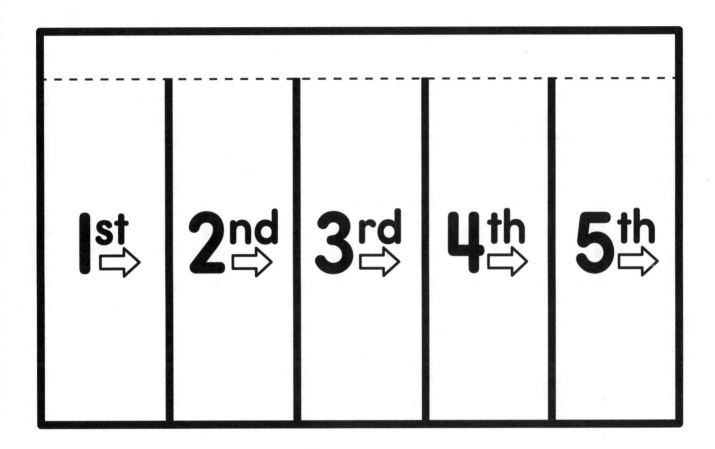

1st ➡ 2nd ➡ 3rd ➡ 4th ➡ 5th ➡

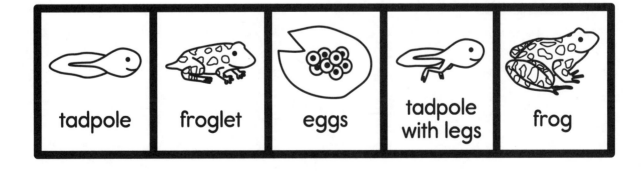

tadpole | froglet | eggs | tadpole with legs | frog

Parts of a Frog

Introduction

Have students act out the movements of a frog. Ask students what body parts they would use to hear with, smell with, eat with, and move with if they were frogs. Draw a Venn diagram on the board. Ask students to compare their body parts with a frog's body parts. Write students' responses in the diagram. Then, use a picture of a frog to describe its body parts.

Creating the Notebook Page

Guide students through the following steps to complete the right-hand page in their notebooks.

1. Add a Table of Contents entry for the Parts of a Frog pages.

2. Cut out the title and glue it to the top of the page.

3. Cut out the frog shutter fold. Apply glue to the back of the center section and attach it to the page.

4. Fold on the dashed lines to create two flaps that fold in to cover the frog diagram.

5. Cut out the word cards. Open the flaps and use the word cards to label the frog diagram. Glue the word cards to the corresponding parts of the frog. Close the flaps. On the front of the book, write *I can name the parts of a frog.*

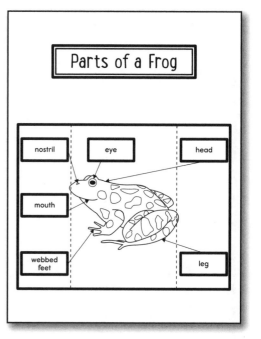

Reflect on Learning

To complete the left-hand page, have students write sentences about the importance of the frog's body parts. For example, *Frogs need webbed feet to swim faster.*

Parts of a Frog

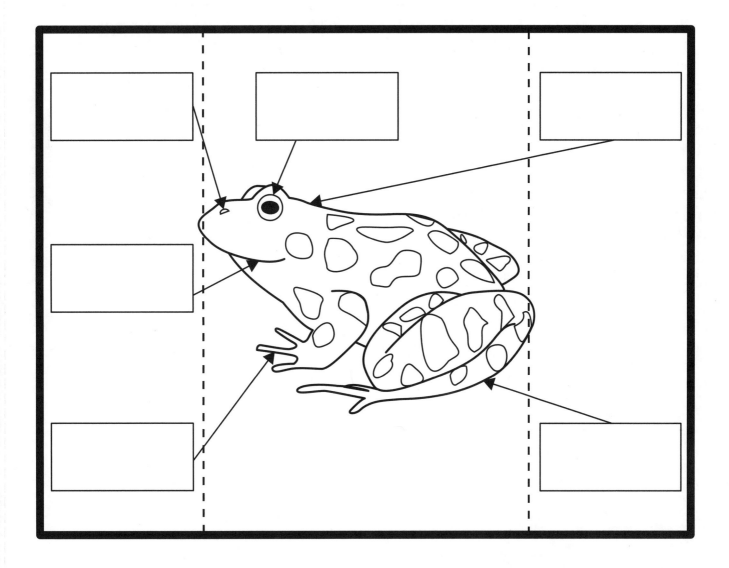

eye	mouth	leg
head	nostril	webbed feet

Animal Habitats

Introduction

Have students look outside and describe where they live (city, country, neighborhood, etc.). Explain that this is called a *habitat*. Discuss how humans need homes, transportation, food, water, clothing, etc., to survive. The places we live provide us with these things. Animals have specific needs as well. They need a habitat that will support their lives. Ask students to name animals and the habitats they live in. Have students describe why each animal may live in that particular habitat. For example, *A whale lives in the ocean because it has fins and swims.*

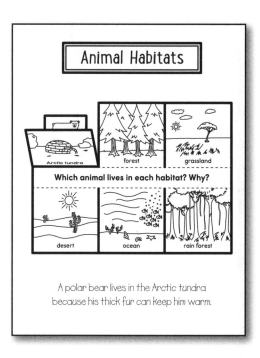

Creating the Notebook Page

Guide students through the following steps to complete the right-hand page in their notebooks.

1. Add a Table of Contents entry for the Animal Habitats pages.

2. Cut out the title and glue it to the top of the page.

3. Cut out the flap book. Cut on the solid lines to create six flaps. Apply glue to the back of the center section and attach it to the page.

4. Cut out the picture cards. Look at each one and decide which habitat the animal would live in. Glue each picture under the correct flap.

5. Choose one of the animals. Below the flap book, write a sentence explaining why the animal lives in that particular habitat.

Reflect on Learning

To complete the left-hand page, have students draw a picture of a habitat. Have students choose an animal that does not live in that habitat. Have them draw what features this animal would need in order to live in the habitat. Finally, have students write a sentence explaining their reasoning.

Animal Habitats

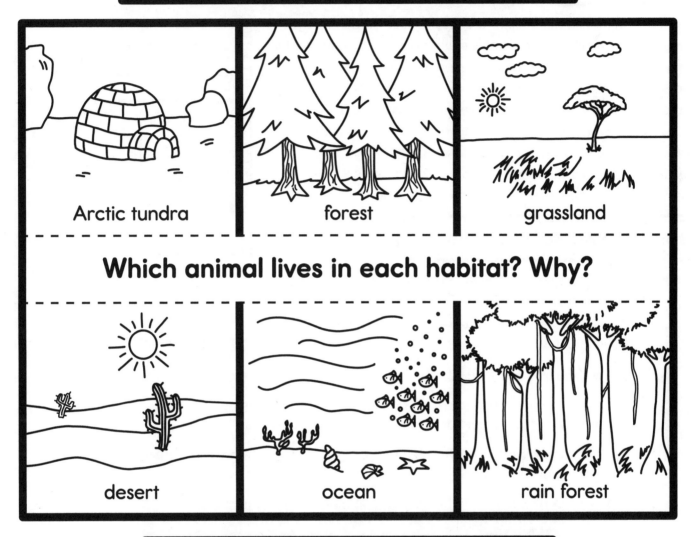

Arctic tundra

forest

grassland

Which animal lives in each habitat? Why?

desert

ocean

rain forest

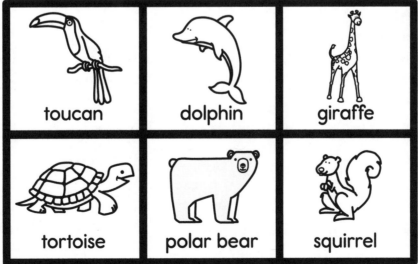

toucan

dolphin

giraffe

tortoise

polar bear

squirrel

Hibernate or Migrate

Introduction

Distribute animal name cards or pictures to each student. Have students discuss what their animals might do to survive the winter. Explain how some animals hibernate, or go into a resting state, and some animals migrate, or move to a different place during the winter. Explain that animals that hibernate eat or store a lot of food in the summer to prepare for winter. Animals that migrate need to look for food or warmer temperatures. Write *Hibernate* and *Migrate* on the board. Have students place their animal pictures under the action they think their animals might do.

Creating the Notebook Page

Guide students through the following steps to complete the right-hand page in their notebooks.

1. Add a Table of Contents entry for the Hibernate or Migrate pages.

2. Cut out the title and glue it to the top of the page.

3. Cut out the *hibernate/migrate* flap book. Cut on the solid line to create two flaps. Apply glue to the back of the top section and attach it to the page.

4. Cut out picture cards. Look at each picture and decide whether the animal hibernates or migrates. Glue each picture under the correct flap.

5. Below each flap, draw another animal that hibernates or migrates.

Reflect on Learning

To complete the left-hand page, have students choose an animal from the right-hand page. Students should write a short story about hibernation or migration from the animal's point of view. Allow time for students to share their work.

Hibernate or Migrate

What do these animals do in the winter?

hibernate	migrate

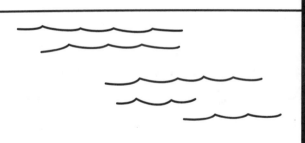

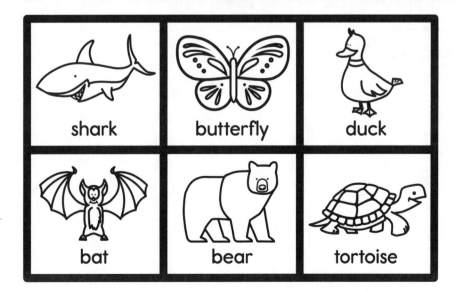

shark	butterfly	duck
bat	bear	tortoise

Animal Mothers and Babies

Introduction

Distribute picture cards of animal babies to half of the class and pictures of matching animal mothers to the other half of the class. Have students walk around the room and ask the other students who have mother animal pictures, "Are you my mother?" After students find their matches, they should discuss how the mother and baby look alike. For example, do they have the same characteristics like webbed feet, mane of hair, etc.? Have the student pairs share the reasons why each mother belongs with her baby.

Creating the Notebook Page

Guide students through the following steps to complete the right-hand page in their notebooks.

1. Add a Table of Contents entry for the Animal Mothers and Babies pages.

2. Cut out the title and glue it to the top of the page.

3. Cut out the flower piece. Cut on the solid lines to create six petal-shaped flaps. Apply glue to the back of the center section and attach it to the page.

4. Cut out the picture cards. Look at each one and decide which mother the baby belongs to. Glue each picture under the correct flap.

5. Choose one of the animal pairs. Below the flower piece, write a sentence about one characteristic that the mother and baby animal share.

Reflect on Learning

To complete the left-hand page, have students create an animal mother and baby collage. Provide students with magazines or newspapers. Have students cut out pictures of animal mothers and their babies. Have them label their pictures with a characteristic each mother and baby share.

Animal Mothers and Babies

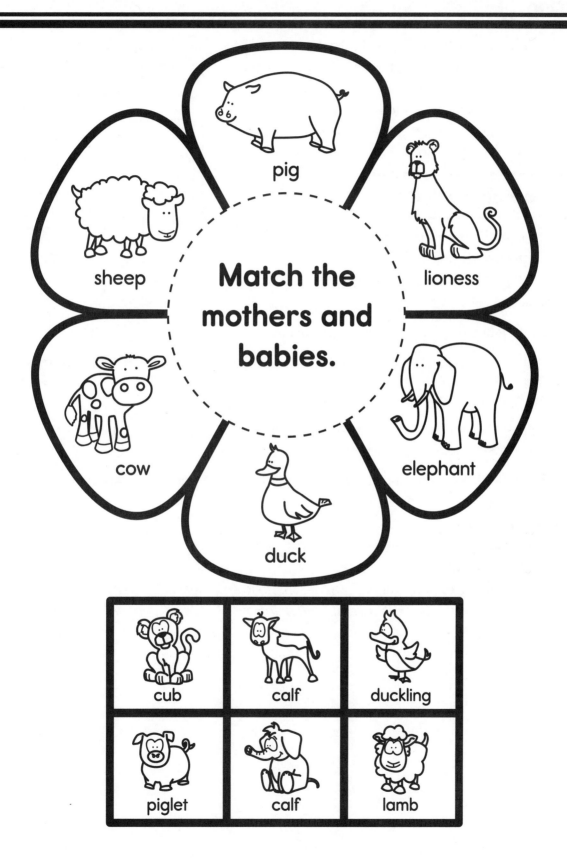

pig

lioness

sheep

Match the mothers and babies.

cow

elephant

duck

cub	calf	duckling
piglet	calf	lamb

Animals and Plants

Introduction

Write the word *Needs* on the board. Below it, list the words *TV, food, water, toys, air,* and *home*. Have students discuss which of these words on the list they need to survive. Have students share their ideas with partners. As a class, discuss wants versus needs. Then, explain that animals and plants also have basic needs to survive. Plants and animals share some, but not all, basic needs.

Creating the Notebook Page

Guide students through the following steps to complete the right-hand page in their notebooks.

1. Add a Table of Contents entry for the Animals and Plants pages.

2. Cut out the title and glue it to the top of the page.

3. Cut out the flap book. Cut on the solid lines to create three flaps. Apply glue to the back of the top section and attach it to the page.

4. Cut out the word cards. Read each word and decide whether the need belongs to an animal, a plant, or both. Glue each word under the correct flap.

5. Below the flap book, draw a picture of a real or imaginary pet along with its needs. Label each of its needs.

Reflect on Learning

To complete the left-hand page, have students answer the following questions: *Why don't animals need soil and sunlight to survive? Why do both animals and plants need water to survive?*

Animals and Plants

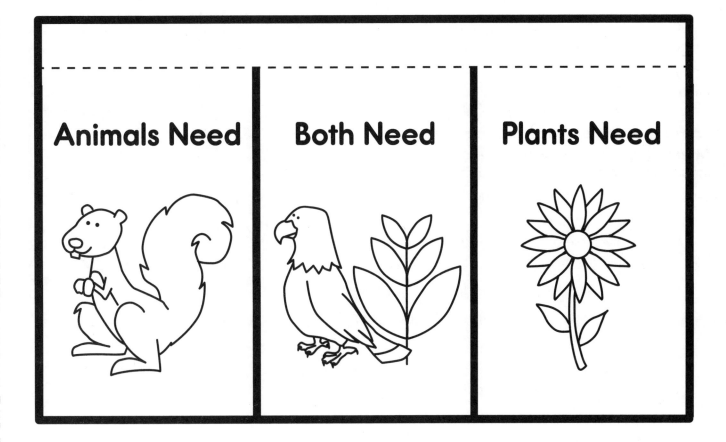

Animals Need

Both Need

Plants Need

| soil | water | food |
| air | sunlight | shelter |

Physical Properties

Introduction

Display a variety of objects such as a book, a pencil, a piece of paper, a pen, and a pair of scissors. Explain that you can sort items by physical properties such as size, texture, weight, color, or temperature. Discuss how objects can be sorted by more than one category because many objects have more than one property. For example, a pair of scissors can be both smooth and cold. Have a volunteer sort the objects by their physical properties and explain his reasoning. Repeat with several different volunteers.

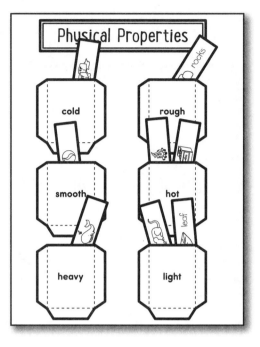

Creating the Notebook Page

Guide students through the following steps to complete the right-hand page in their notebooks.

1. Add a Table of Contents entry for the Physical Properties pages.

2. Cut out the title and glue it to the top of the page.

3. Cut out the pockets. Apply glue to the back of the tabs and attach them to the page to create three rows of two pockets each.

4. Cut out the picture strips. Look at each picture and sort by physical properties. Place the picture strips in the correct pockets.

5. Cut out the two blank strips. On the strips, write or draw two more objects that have one of the physical properties on the pockets. Place the strips in the correct pockets.

6. After sorting the objects by properties, look at the picture strips again and compare your objects. Decide whether they can be moved into different physical property pockets.

Reflect on Learning

To complete the left-hand page, have students use the pictures from the right-hand page to write comparison statements about physical properties. For example, *An ice cube is lighter than a marble.*

Physical Properties

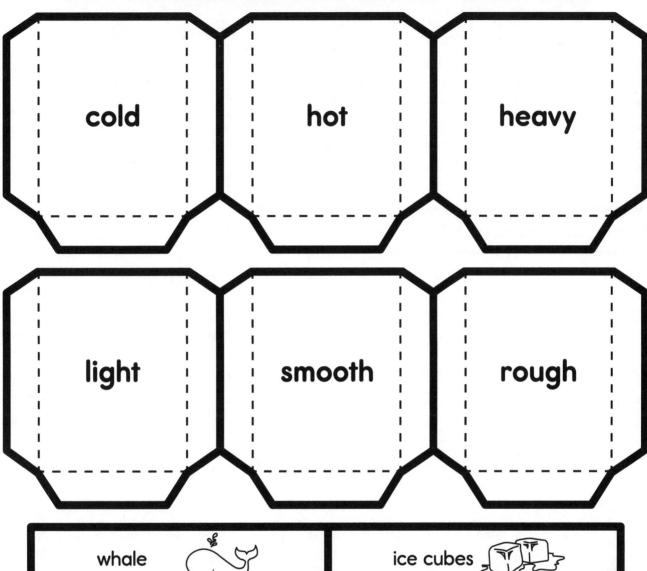

cold	hot
heavy	
light	smooth
rough	

whale		ice cubes	
mouse		marble	
fire		oven	

States of Matter

Introduction

Write the words *solid, liquid,* and *gas* on the board. Have students share examples of each (door, water, air, etc.). List their ideas under each category. Then, have students stand and model each state of matter. Have students model solids by standing closely together in rows. Students can move together as a group, but must stay in formation. Have students model liquids by lining up, linking their hands, and making a wave motion along the line. Have students model gases by moving about the room but never touching each other.

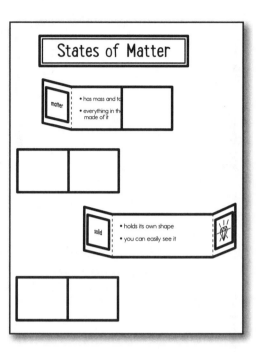

Creating the Notebook Page

Guide students through the following steps to complete the right-hand page in their notebooks.

1. Add a Table of Contents entry for the States of Matter pages.

2. Cut out the title and glue it to the top of the page.

3. Cut out the four shutter folds. Apply glue to the back of the center sections and attach them to the page one below the other. Fold on the dashed lines to create two flaps on each shutter fold that fold in to cover the text.

4. Cut out the picture cards and word cards. Read each definition on the inside of the shutter fold. On the left side, glue the correct word to match the definition. On the right side, glue the correct picture to match the definition.

5. With a partner, read and discuss the definitions on each shutter fold. Then, give another example of a solid, liquid, and gas for each one. Write it on the page beside each shutter fold.

Reflect on Learning

To complete the left-hand page, have students draw lines to make three columns labeled *solids, liquids,* and *gases*. Provide students with magazines or newspapers. Then, have students cut out pictures of objects that represent the different states of matter. Students should glue the pictures into the correct columns.

States of Matter

- has mass and takes up space
- everything in the world is made of it

- takes the shape of its container
- you can pour it

- holds its own shape
- you can easily see it

- does not have a shape
- hard to see

matter	liquid	gas	solid

Changes in Matter

Introduction

Review the three states of matter. Explain that matter can change when it is heated or cooled. Ask students what happens to water when it freezes. (It becomes ice.) Explain that as matter changes temperature, it turns into a different state of matter. Display ice cubes and a cup of hot water. Ask students to predict what will happen to the ice cubes when they are placed in the water. Place the ice cubes in the water to demonstrate how the ice melts.

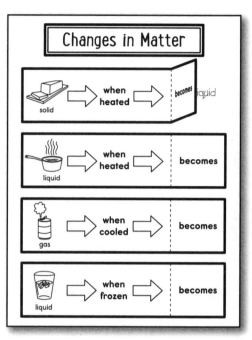

Creating the Notebook Page

Guide students through the following steps to complete the right-hand page in their notebooks.

1. Add a Table of Contents entry for the Changes in Matter pages.

2. Cut out the title and glue it to the top of the page.

3. Cut out the four flaps. Apply glue to the back of the left section of each flap and attach them to the page, one below the other.

4. Look at the objects on the front of the flaps. Think about how each object will change when it is heated or cooled. Complete the phrase by writing which state of matter each object becomes under the flap.

Reflect on Learning

To complete the left-hand page, have students draw a picture to demonstrate what happens to an ice-cream cone on a hot day. Students should write a sentence to explain their drawings.

Changes in Matter

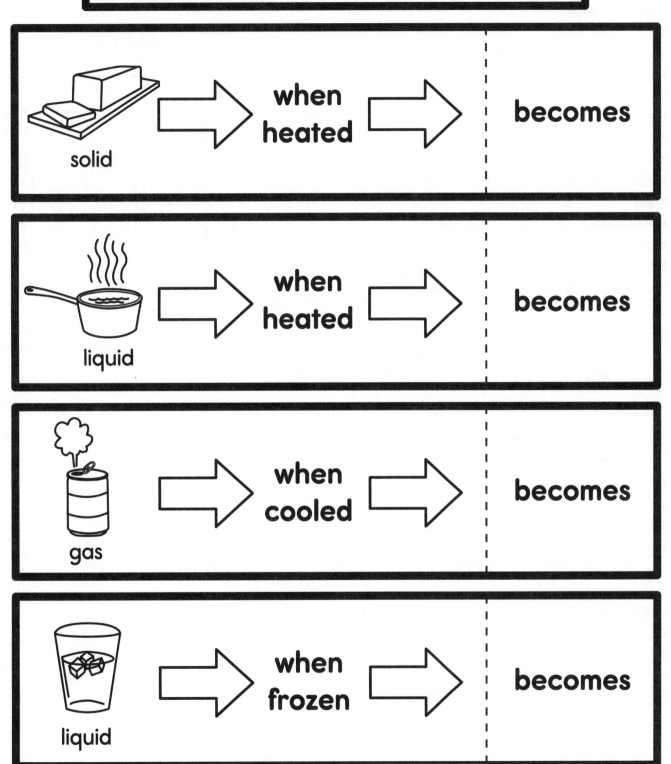

solid → when heated → becomes

liquid → when heated → becomes

gas → when cooled → becomes

liquid → when frozen → becomes

Sink or Float

Introduction

Draw a T-chart on the board labeled *sink* and *float*. Display a paper clip, a crayon, an eraser, a cotton ball, a toothpick, and a plastic cap. Ask students to predict which items will sink and which will float. Write their predictions on the board. Have volunteers place objects one at a time in a bowl filled with water to test which items will sink and which will float. After the experiment, ask students to draw conclusions as to why certain objects floated and others did not. Explain to students that objects that have more mass will sink and objects that have less mass have buoyancy, meaning that they will float.

Creating the Notebook Page

Guide students through the following steps to complete the right-hand page in their notebooks.

1. Add a Table of Contents entry for the Sink or Float pages.

2. Cut out the title and glue it to the top of the page.

3. Cut out the *Buoyancy is* definition piece. Glue it below the title.

4. Complete the definition of *buoyancy*. (Buoyancy is the ability to **float** in liquid.)

5. Cut out the *float and sink* accordion folds. Fold on the dashed lines, alternating the fold direction so that the *float and sink* sections are on top. Apply glue to the back of the *These items* sections and attach them side-by-side near the center of the page.

6. Cut out the picture cards. Look at each picture and decide which objects sink and which objects float. Glue each picture onto the correct accordion piece.

Reflect on Learning

To complete the left-hand page, have students draw a horizontal line to divide their pages into two sections. Have students label the top section *float* and the bottom section *sink*. Students should write or draw pictures of more items that will float and sink in each section.

Sink or Float

Buoyancy is the ability to _____ in liquid.

These items				float
These items				sink

leaf	apple	key
pencil	spoon	penny

Forms of Energy

Introduction

Have a student make a shadow puppet on the wall while the teacher holds a flashlight. Have another student knock on the door and another student rub his hands together. Explain that all of these students used a form of energy. Energy is the ability to do work. Explain that they demonstrated light energy, sound energy, and heat energy. Have the class discuss which action used which form of energy.

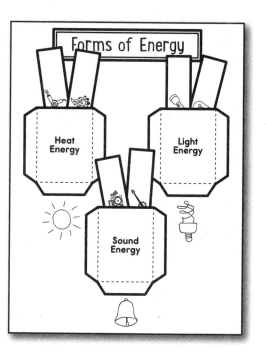

Creating the Notebook Page

Guide students through the following steps to complete the right-hand page in their notebooks.

1. Add a Table of Contents entry for the Forms of Energy pages.

2. Cut out the title and glue it to the top of the page.

3. Cut out the pockets. Apply glue to the back of the tabs and attach them to the page.

4. Cut out the picture strips. Decide which form of energy each picture represents. Place the picture strips into the correct pockets.

5. Below each pocket, draw a picture that represents another example of each form of energy.

Reflect on Learning

To complete the left-hand page, have students draw lines to divide their pages into three sections. Have students label each section *light, heat,* and *sound.* Provide students with magazines or newspapers. Then, have students cut out pictures of objects that represent different forms of energy. Have them glue the pictures into the correct columns.

Forms of Energy

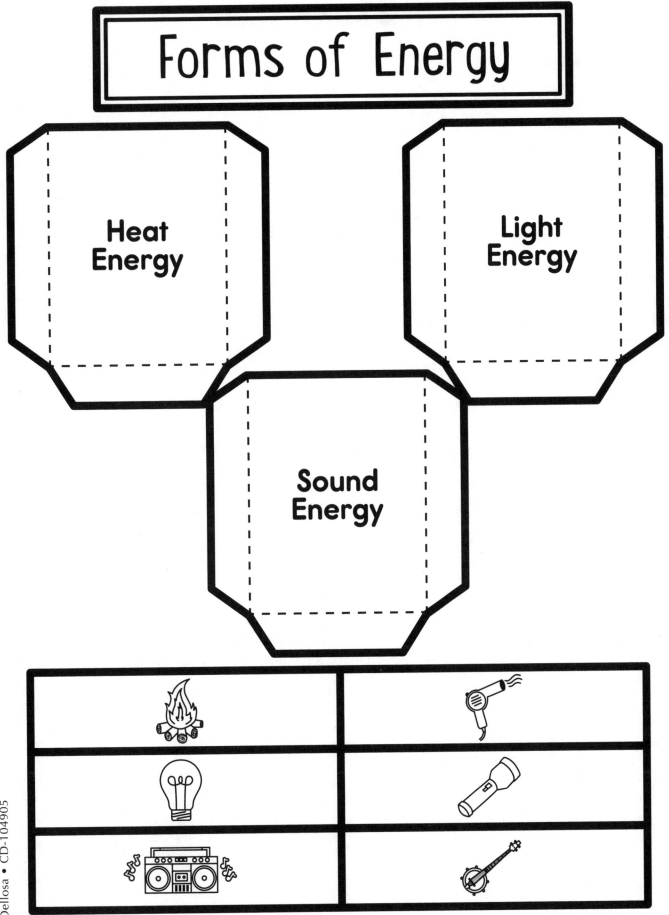

Heat Energy

Light Energy

Sound Energy

Sound

Introduction

Have students clap their hands, and then tap the table. Ask students which sound was louder. Explain that sound comes from vibrations. When we clap our hands, we make a vibration. Our hands are small and solid. The sound is relatively small. When we tap the table harder or softer, it makes a larger or smaller vibration, which makes a louder or softer sound. Explain that the amount and speed of vibration allows sound to become louder or more high-pitched. Discuss the difference between a ship's horn and an ambulance's siren. They both vibrate, but they are made differently, so they create different sounds.

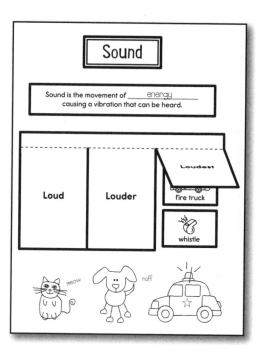

Creating the Notebook Page

Guide students through the following steps to complete the right-hand page in their notebooks.

1. Add a Table of Contents entry for the Sound pages.

2. Cut out the title and glue it to the top of the page.

3. Cut out the definition piece. Glue it below the title.

4. Complete the definition of *sound*. (Sound is the movement of **energy**, causing a vibration that can be heard.)

5. Cut out the flap book. Cut on the solid lines to create three flaps. Apply glue to the back of the top section and attach it to the page.

6. Cut out the picture cards. Look at the pictures, compare the objects, and decide which objects are loud, louder, or loudest. Glue each picture under the correct flap.

7. Write or draw more objects to compare their sounds below the *loud, louder,* and *loudest* flaps.

Reflect on Learning

To complete the left-hand page, have students use the pictures from the right-hand page to write comparison statements about sound. For example, *A fire truck is louder than an alarm clock.*

Sound

Sound is the movement of _____,
causing a vibration that can be heard.

Loud	Louder	Loudest

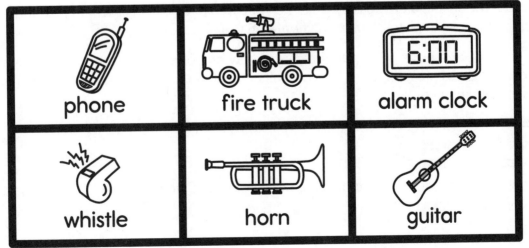

phone | fire truck | alarm clock

whistle | horn | guitar

Light

Each group of students will need a flashlight, black construction paper, and an empty cardboard tube to complete the introduction activity.

Introduction

Divide students into small groups. Using a flashlight, black construction paper, and a cardboard tube, have students experiment with various objects to determine if light will pass through the objects. For example, have a student place a flashlight at one end of the cardboard tube. Then, have another student place a piece of notebook paper at the other end of the tube. Have a third student hold the black paper a few feet behind the notebook paper. Have students determine if the light passed through the notebook paper onto the black paper. Have each group of students experiment with different objects between the cardboard tube and the black paper, such as a plastic resealable bag, a book, a chair, a plastic bottle, etc.

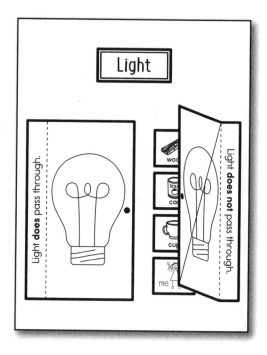

Creating the Notebook Page

Guide students through the following steps to complete the right-hand page in their notebooks.

1. Add a Table of Contents entry for the Light pages.

2. Cut out the title and glue it to the top of the page.

3. Cut out the lightbulb flaps. Apply glue to the back of the narrow right or left section of each flap. Attach the flaps to the page, placing them side by side so that the inside edges of the pieces align.

4. Cut out the six picture cards. Look at each one and decide if light would pass through the object. Glue each picture under the correct flap.

5. Cut out the two blank cards. On the cards, draw one object from the introduction that allowed light to pass through it and one object that did not. Glue the pictures under the corresponding flaps.

Reflect on Learning

To complete the left-hand page, have students draw a flashlight. Students should write or draw two more objects that would allow light to pass through them.

Light

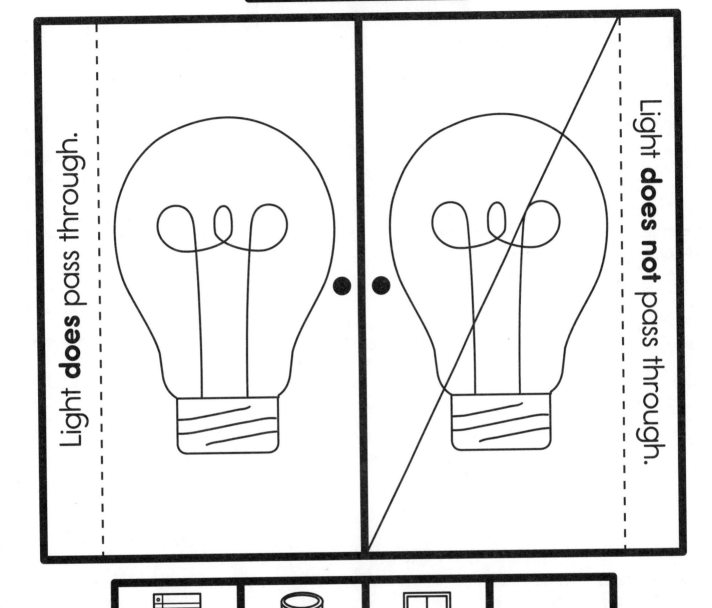

Light **does** pass through.

Light **does not** pass through.

paper	can	window
wax paper	wood	cup

Motion

Introduction

Divide students into four groups. Have one group move in a zigzag line, another group move back and forth, another group move in a circle, and the last group walk in a straight line. Explain that objects can move in many ways. Have students discuss why an object would need to move in a certain way. Then, have three students move across the room in different ways. For example, have one student hop, another walk, and another crawl. Ask students which way was the fastest and which way was the slowest. Explain that different kinds of movement changes the speed of the object.

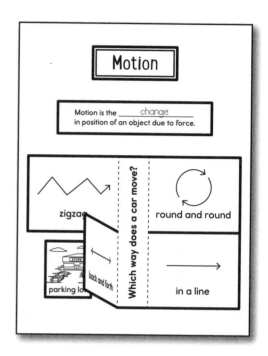

Creating the Notebook Page

Guide students through the following steps to complete the right-hand page in their notebooks.

1. Add a Table of Contents entry for the Motion pages.

2. Cut out the title and glue it to the top of the page.

3. Cut out the definition piece and glue it below the title.

4. Complete the definition of *motion*. (Motion is the **change** in position of an object due to force.)

5. Cut out the flap book. Cut on the solid lines to create four flaps. Apply glue to the back of the center section and attach it to the page.

6. Cut out the picture cards. Look at each one and decide which type of motion a car would use in that setting. Glue each picture under the correct flap.

Reflect on Learning

To complete the left-hand page, have students design a skate park with different kinds of ramps that would allow a skater to move in many different ways. For example, back and forth, zigzag, or fast and slow. Have students label each ramp with the type of movement the ramp represents.

Motion

Motion is the _____ in position of an object due to force.

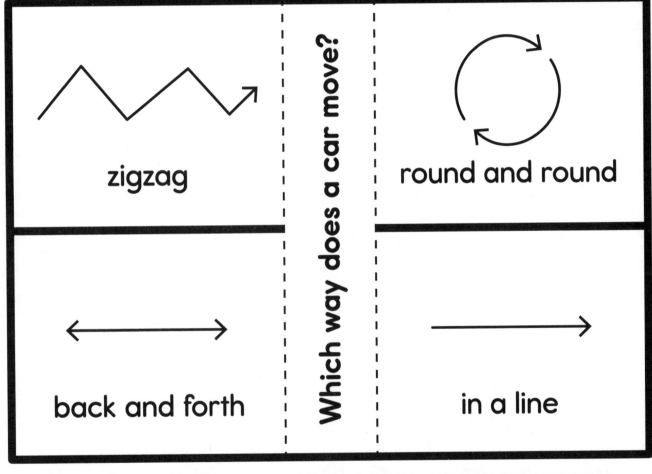

zigzag

Which way does a car move?

round and round

back and forth

in a line

mountain

racetrack

parking lot

street

Push or Pull

© Carson-Dellosa • CD-104905

Introduction

Discuss how some objects need to be pushed or pulled in order to move. Explain that how much energy we put into the push or pull can make the object move differently. This is called *force*. Display a ball and ask students to predict whether or not pushing or pulling the ball would make it go faster. Record students' responses on the board. Have a student push the ball and another student pull the ball. Have students compare and discuss their predictions.

Creating the Notebook Page

Guide students through the following steps to complete the right-hand page in their notebooks.

1. Add a Table of Contents entry for the Push or Pull pages.

2. Cut out the title and glue it to the top of the page.

3. Cut out the definition piece and glue it below the title.

4. Complete the definition. (**Force** means using energy to do work. Pushing and pulling are types of work.)

5. Cut out each flap. Apply glue to the back of the top section of each flap and attach them to the page.

6. Look at the picture on each flap. Decide whether the picture represents pushing or pulling. Write *push* or *pull* under each flap.

Reflect on Learning

To complete the left-hand page, have students draw a horizontal line to divide their pages into two sections. Have them label the top section *pull* and the bottom section *push*. In each section, have students write or draw objects that can be pushed or pulled.

Push or Pull

_____ means using energy to do work. Pushing and pulling are types of work.

Magnetism

Each group of students will need magnets, metal objects, and nonmetal objects to complete the introduction activity.

Introduction

Define magnetism as a force that can push or pull objects. Divide students into groups. Give each group a magnet and objects such as paper clips, bolts, buttons, erasers, etc. Have each group experiment with the magnets to determine which objects are magnetic. Have students share their results. As a class, discuss why some of the objects were magnetic and some were not.

Caution: Keep small magnets and small pieces containing magnets away from young children who might mistakenly or intentionally swallow them. Seek immediate medical attention if you suspect a child may have swallowed a magnet.

Creating the Notebook Page

Guide students through the following steps to complete the right-hand page in their notebooks.

1. Add a Table of Contents entry for the Magnetism pages.

2. Cut out the title and glue it to the top of the page.

3. Cut out the definition piece. Glue it below the title.

4. Complete the definition of *magnetism* (a force that can **push** or **pull** objects).

5. Cut out the *Magnetic* piece. Glue it to the page below the definition piece.

6. Cut out the *Not Magnetic* piece and glue it below the *Magnetic* piece.

7. Cut out the picture cards. Look at each picture and decide if the object would be pulled or pushed when held near a magnet (magnetic). Glue the pictures of the objects that would be magnetic on top of the *Magnetic* piece. Glue the pictures of the objects that would not be magnetic below the *Not Magnetic* piece.

Reflect on Learning

To complete the left-hand page, have students write a summary statement of why magnets attract only specific things. Have students discuss their ideas with partners.

Magnetism

a force that can _____
or _____ objects

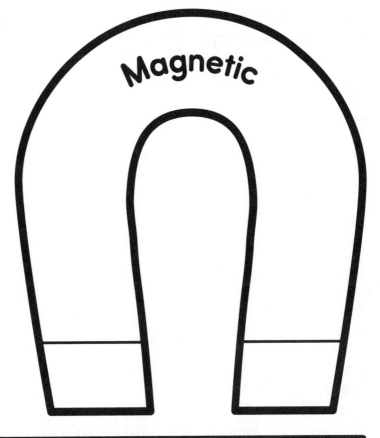

Magnetic

Not Magnetic

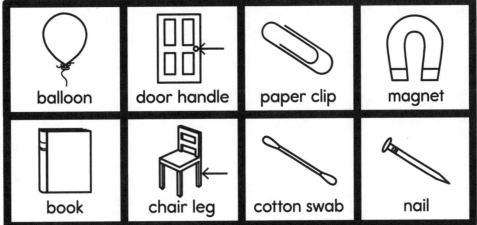

| balloon | door handle | paper clip | magnet |
| book | chair leg | cotton swab | nail |

Day or Night

Introduction

Have students discuss with partners the following question: *How does the sky look at nighttime and how does it look in the daytime?* Draw a T-chart on the board labeled *Day* and *Night*. Have students share their responses and list them on the chart. Explain how the sun gives us light during the day. Discuss how, as Earth rotates away from the sun, the sky looks dark at night.

Creating the Notebook Page

Guide students through the following steps to complete the right-hand page in their notebooks.

1. Add a Table of Contents entry for the Day or Night pages.

2. Cut out the title and glue it to the top of the page.

3. Cut out the flap book. Cut on the solid line to create two flaps. Apply glue to the back of the top section and attach it to the page.

4. Cut out the picture cards. Look at each picture and decide whether it is an object that can be seen during the day or at night. Glue the pictures on top of the corresponding flaps and add details to create a daytime scene and a nighttime scene.

5. Under each flap, write a sentence to explain the scene.

Reflect on Learning

To complete the left-hand page, have students draw a horizontal line to divide their pages into two sections. Have them label the top section *day* and the bottom section *night*. In each section, have students write or draw objects that can be seen in the sky in the day and objects that can be seen in the sky at night.

Day or Night

What do you see in the sky?

day	night

Effects of the Sun

Introduction

Have students stand outside or stand by a window on a sunny day. Ask students if they can feel the warmth from the sun's heat. Then, explain that the sun is the largest star in our solar system and Earth orbits around it. Without the sun, Earth would not be able to exist. Ask students to share ideas of how the sun helps us and how it can harm us. List students' ideas on the board.

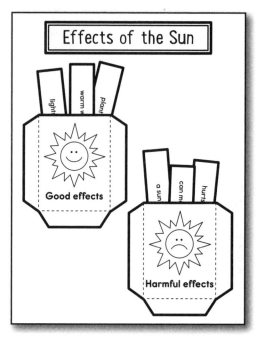

Creating the Notebook Page

Guide students through the following steps to complete the right-hand page in their notebooks.

1. Add a Table of Contents entry for the Effects of the Sun pages.

2. Cut out the title and glue it to the top of the page.

3. Cut out the *Good effects* and *Harmful effects* pockets. Apply glue to the back of the tabs and attach them to the page to create two pockets.

4. Cut out the effect strips. Read each effect and decide whether it is a good effect from the sun or a harmful effect. Place each strip inside the correct pocket.

Reflect on Learning

To complete the left-hand page, have students draw pictures or list objects we use to protect ourselves from the harmful effects of the sun, such as hats, sunglasses, and sunscreen.

© Carson-Dellosa • CD-104905

Effects of the Sun

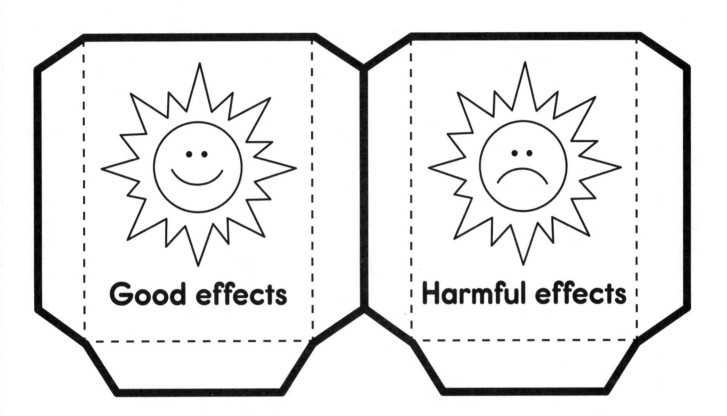

Good effects

Harmful effects

a sunburn	warm weather
plant food	hurts your eyes
can make you too hot	lights the sky

Changes in the Moon

Each student will need a brass paper fastener to complete the right side of the page and five chocolate cream sandwich cookies to complete the introduction activity.

Introduction

Explain that we can see the moon because the sun's light reflects off of it. Discuss how, as the moon orbits Earth, it moves away from the sun. Provide each student with five chocolate cream sandwich cookies. Have students separate the sandwich cookies to demonstrate five phases of the moon as follows: A full moon (all cream), a gibbous moon (scrape off a small section of cream), a half moon (scrape off half of the cream), a crescent moon (scrape cream into a crescent), and a new moon (no cream).

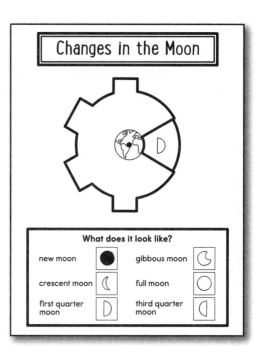

Creating the Notebook Page

Guide students through the following steps to complete the right-hand page in their notebooks.

1. Add a Table of Contents entry for the Changes in the Moon pages.

2. Cut out the title and glue it to the top of the page.

3. Cut out the moon cycle circle and the tabbed piece. Place the tabbed piece on top of the moon cycle circle. Push a brass paper fastener through the center dots of the circles to attach them. It may be helpful to create the hole in each piece separately first.

4. Apply glue to the back of the top piece's tabs and attach it to the page below the title. The brass paper fastener should not go through the page, and the moon cycle circle beneath should spin freely.

5. Move the circle so that it displays each phase of the moon cycle. Select one phase. Decide which phase would occur before and after that phase. Check to see if you are correct by moving the circle and viewing the phases before and after it.

6. Cut out the *What does it look like?* piece and glue it to the bottom of the page. Refer to the moon cycle circle to help you draw the changes in the moon for each phase.

Reflect on Learning

To complete the left-hand page, have students draw lines to divide their pages into four sections. Have students return to the page every day for the rest of the week and draw what the moon looked like the night before. Have students label their pictures with the correct moon phases.

Changes in the Moon

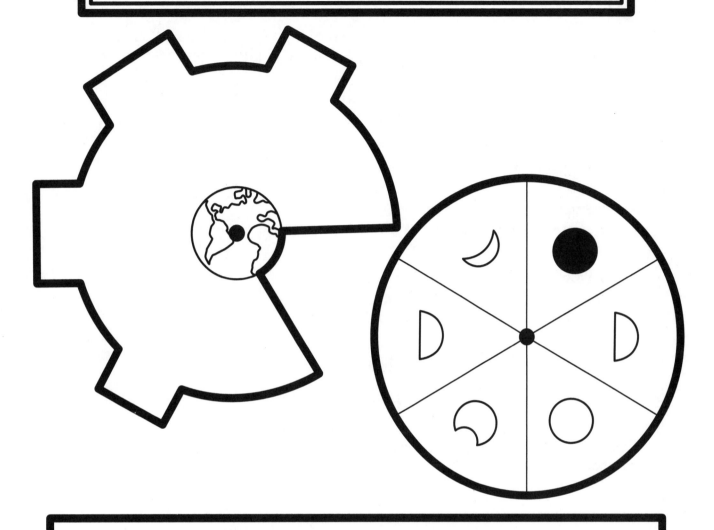

What does it look like?

new moon ☐

gibbous moon ☐

crescent moon ☐

full moon ☐

first quarter moon ☐

third quarter moon ☐

Earth's Natural Resources

Introduction

Draw a concept bubble map on the board. In the center bubble, write *Natural Resources.* Explain that we use things called natural resources from the earth in order to live. Have students brainstorm some natural resources. Write their answers in the bubble map. Explain that Earth gives us water, soil, plants, and animals. Have students work with partners. Partners should discuss the benefits of each of these resources and brainstorm items they provide us with, such as honey, rivers, wood, etc.

Creating the Notebook Page

Guide students through the following steps to complete the right-hand page in their notebooks.

1. Add a Table of Contents entry for the Earth's Natural Resources pages.

2. Cut out the title and glue it to the top of the page.

3. Cut out the resource pockets. Apply glue to the back of the tabs and attach them to the page.

4. Cut out the eight word strips. On the back of each strip draw the object that matches the word on the front.

5. Decide which objects come from which of Earth's resources. Place the word strips inside the correct pockets.

6. Cut out the four blank strips. Write and draw four more objects that come from Earth's natural resources on the strips. Place them inside the correct pockets.

Reflect on Learning

To complete the left-hand page, have students draw lines to divide their pages into four sections and label them *water, soil, plants,* and *animals.* Then, send students on a natural resource hunt. Ask them to find pictures in books or objects outside that are a part of Earth's natural resources. Have students write words or draw pictures in the corresponding sections.

Caution: Before beginning any nature activity, ask families' permission and inquire about students' plant and animal allergies. Remind students not to touch plants or animals during the activity.

Earth's Natural Resources

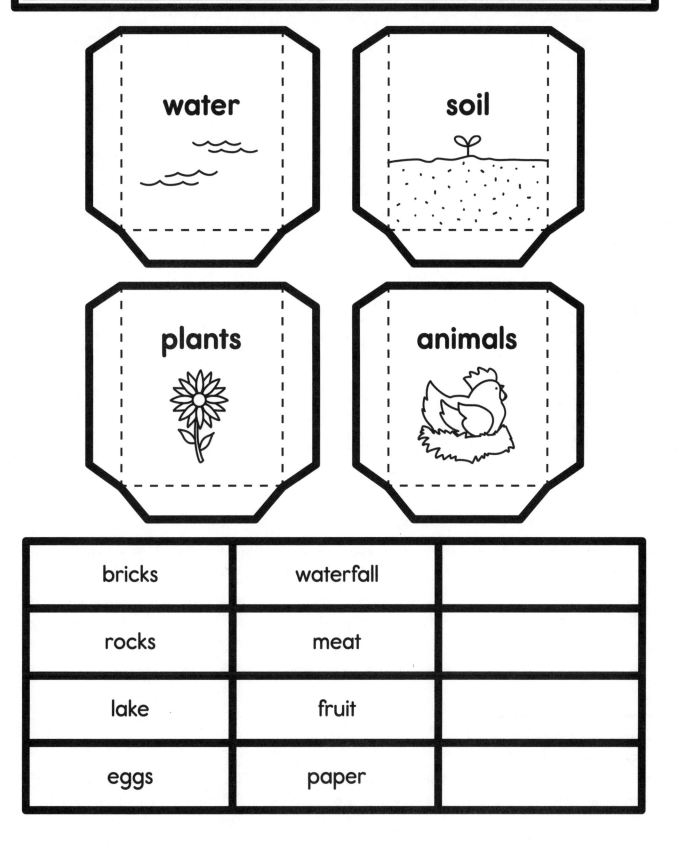

water	soil
plants	animals

bricks	waterfall	
rocks	meat	
lake	fruit	
eggs	paper	

Soil

Each group of students will need two small bags of clean soil, a paper plate, and a small cup of water to complete the introduction activity.

Introduction

Discuss different types of soil such as sand, humus, and clay. Explain that soil is made up of many things, including tiny rocks that have broken down over time. Divide students into small groups. Give each group two bags of clean soil and a paper plate. Allow the students to pour one of the bags onto the plate. Ask students to investigate their soil. What does it look and feel like? What do they think it will absorb? Distribute small cups of water to each group. Allow students to pour the water on top of the soil in the remaining bag and observe the results. Provide materials such as paper, rocks, and plastic for students to experiment with to determine if soil will absorb these other types of materials.

Caution: Before beginning any nature activity, ask families' permission and inquire about students' plant and animal allergies. Remind students not to touch plants or animals during the activity.

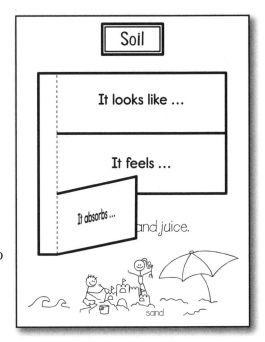

Creating the Notebook Page

Guide students through the following steps to complete the right-hand page in their notebooks.

1. Add a Table of Contents entry for the Soil pages.

2. Cut out the title and glue it to the top of the page.

3. Cut out the flap book. Cut on the solid lines to create three flaps. Apply glue to the back of the left section of the flap book and attach it to the page below the title.

4. From the introduction experiment, answer the following questions: *What does soil look like? What does soil feel like? What does soil absorb?* Write the answers to the questions under the correct flaps.

5. Below the flap book, draw a scene of a place where you might find a type of soil. Label the soil.

Reflect on Learning

To complete the left-hand page, have students use word clues from the right-hand page to write summary statements about soil. For example, *Soil absorbs water but it does not absorb plastic.*

Soil

It looks like ...

It feels ...

It absorbs ...

Wind

Introduction

Display a fan. Place several objects, such as a pen cap, a glue bottle, and a piece of paper, in front of the fan. Have students predict which objects will be moved as the fan is turned on. Write their predictions on the board. Turn on the fan and have students observe which objects moved. Write these objects on the board and compare them to the students' predictions. Explain that the fan takes the air around us and pulls it in a specific direction. Just like the fan, the earth pulls the air in different directions. Explain that wind is air that is moving.

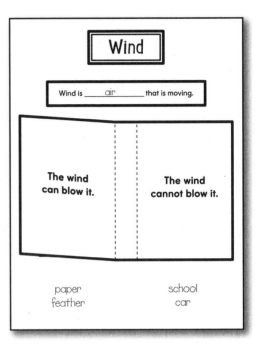

Creating the Notebook Page

Guide students through the following steps to complete the right-hand page in their notebooks.

1. Add a Table of Contents entry for the Wind pages.

2. Cut out the title and glue it to the top of the page.

3. Cut out the definition piece and glue it below the title.

4. Complete the definition of *wind*. (Wind is **air** that is moving.)

5. Cut out the flap book. Apply glue to the back of the center section and attach it to the page.

6. Cut out the picture cards. Look at each object and decide whether the wind would or would not blow it. Glue each picture under the correct flap.

7. Below each flap, draw or list at least one more object that the wind can blow and cannot blow.

Reflect on Learning

To complete the left-hand page, have students write sentences or draw pictures to support the statement *Wind is a force* (it can do work, like pushing or pulling an object).

Wind

Wind is _____ that is moving.

| The wind can blow it. | The wind cannot blow it. |

Bodies of Water

Introduction

Display a glass of water. Ask students to describe places that water comes from. Then, draw, label, and describe four types of bodies of water (lakes, rivers, oceans, and streams) on the board. Explain how each body of water has different uses and can form in different parts of the earth. Then, distribute self-stick notes with various water activities listed, such as *boating, fishing, swimming,* and *water-skiing to* several volunteers. Have each volunteer come to the board and place their activity on a body of water that the activity could occur in.

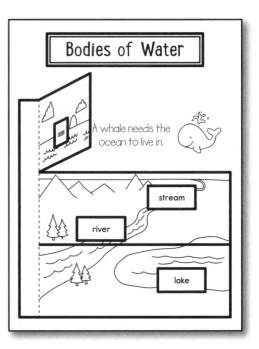

Creating the Notebook Page

Guide students through the following steps to complete the right-hand page in their notebooks.

1. Add a Table of Contents entry for the Bodies of Water pages.

2. Cut out the title and glue it to the top of the page.

3. Cut out the flap book. Cut on the solid lines to create three flaps. Apply glue to the back of the left section and attach it to the page.

4. Cut out the word cards. Read each word and decide which body of water it names. Glue the word card onto the correct section of the flap book to create a diagram.

5. Under each flap, draw a picture of an activity that could take place in that body of water or an animal that would live in that body of water.

Reflect on Learning

To complete the left-hand page, have students answer the following questions: *What is your favorite type of body of water? How is it different than other bodies of water?* Students should draw pictures to illustrate their sentences.

Bodies of Water

| lake | river | stream | ocean |

Water Cycle

Each student will need a brass paper fastener to complete the right side of the page.

Introduction

Pour water into a small cup. Ask students what happens to this water if no one drinks it. Have students discuss with partners what they think will happen. Allow partners to share their ideas. Then, explain that the water will slowly disappear and that this process, called *evaporation,* is one part of the water cycle. Discuss the concepts of condensation, and precipitation. Draw a circle on the board and explain that this process happens over and over again.

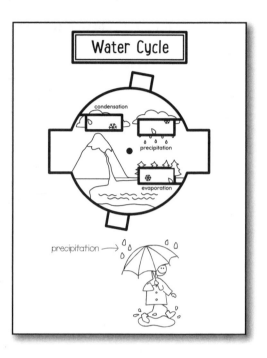

Creating the Notebook Page

Guide students through the following steps to complete the right-hand page in their notebooks.

1. Add a Table of Contents entry for the Water Cycle pages.

2. Cut out the title and glue it to the top of the page.

3. Cut out the water cycle piece. Cut on the solid lines and remove the paper to create three rectangular viewing boxes. Cut out the snow and raindrop piece.

4. Place the water cycle piece on top of the snow and raindrop piece. Push a brass paper fastener through the center dots of the circles to attach them. It may be helpful to create the hole in each piece separately first.

5. Apply glue to the back of the top piece's tabs and attach it to the page below the title. The brass paper fastener should not go through the page, and the snow and raindrop piece beneath it should move freely back and forth between the two tabs.

6. Slowly move the snow and raindrop piece between the side tabs of the water cycle piece to demonstrate the movement of water through the water cycle.

7. Below the water cycle piece, draw a picture of one or more parts of the water cycle. Label the picture with the name of the part or parts of the water cycle it represents.

Reflect on Learning

To complete the left-hand page, have students list the steps of the water cycle in order. Have students draw arrows between the steps to show the correct order.

Water Cycle

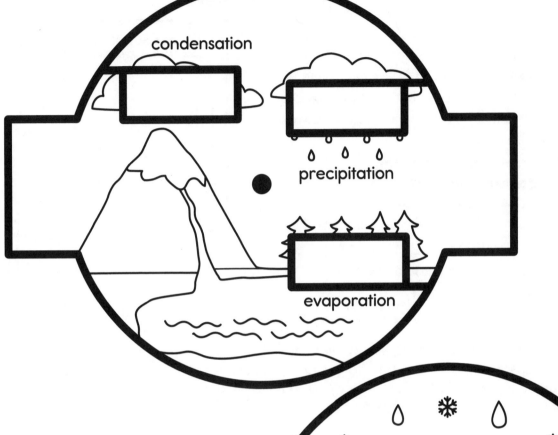

condensation

precipitation

evaporation

Seasonal Changes

Introduction

Write the word *seasons* on the board. Ask students to name the four seasons and list them on the board. Provide students with pictures of seasonal weather. Have students match their pictures to the correct season. Then, have students describe the signs of the different seasons. For example, *Colorful leaves fall on the ground in autumn.* Explain that as the seasons change our needs change. Discuss how seasonal weather dictates what clothes we wear and what activities we can do outside.

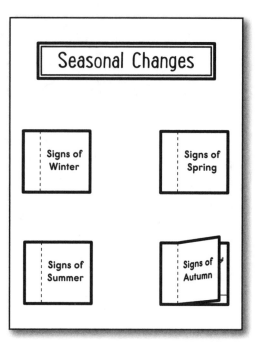

Creating the Notebook Page

Guide students through the following steps to complete the right-hand page in their notebooks.

1. Add a Table of Contents entry for the Seasonal Changes pages.

2. Cut out the title and glue it to the top of the page.

3. Cut out the three flaps of the *Signs of Winter* book. Apply glue to the gray glue sections and place the flaps on top of one another to create a stacked three-flap book. The picture flap should be on top of the blank flap. Apply glue to the back of the left section of the book and attach it to the top left side of the page.

4. Repeat step 3 for all of the *Signs of* books, attaching them to the page in two rows of two.

5. Read the title of each book and look at the first picture. Then, draw a picture of what you would wear in each season on the blank flap. Under the blank flap, draw a picture of an activity you would do in that season.

Reflect on Learning

To complete the left-hand page, have each student create a bar graph or picture graph with the four seasons. Have students label their graphs *The Seasons*. Display pictures such as the seasonal weather pictures from the introduction activity. Have students tally how many pictures relate to each season and then graph the data.

Seasonal Changes

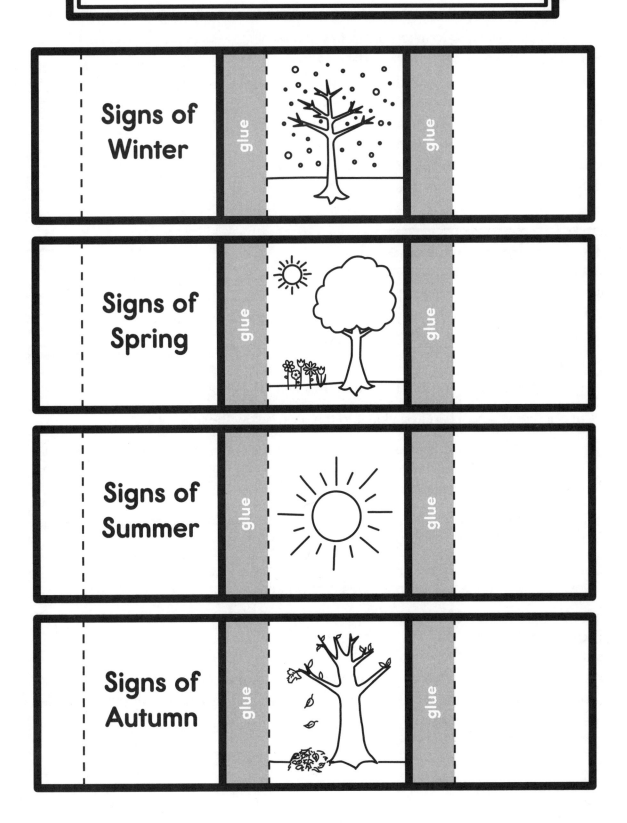

Signs of Winter   glue   glue

Signs of Spring   glue   glue

Signs of Summer   glue   glue

Signs of Autumn   glue   glue

What's the Weather?

Introduction

Display a picture of an extended weather forecast from a local newspaper. Explain that the weather changes daily. Discuss weather terms and the differences between hot and cold, clear and cloudy, calm and windy, rainy and icy. Have students look outside to determine the current weather. Guide students to use weather terms to describe the day's weather. List their responses on the board. Then, have each student draw a picture of the current weather conditions and write a sentence to describe her picture.

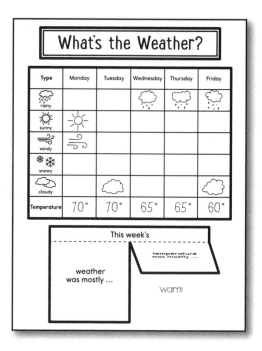

Creating the Notebook Page

Guide students through the following steps to complete the right-hand page in their notebooks.

1. Add a Table of Contents entry for the What's the Weather? pages.

2. Cut out the title and glue it to the top of the page.

3. Cut out the weather chart and glue it to the page below the title.

4. Look at the types of weather listed on the chart. Color or draw in the space in the chart for the current day's weather. Write the current temperature at the bottom of the chart. Record the weather and temperature each day for the next four days.

5. Cut out the flap book. Cut on the solid line to create two flaps. Apply glue to the back of the top section and attach it to the bottom of the page.

6. At the end of the week, use the chart to summarize the weather and temperature for the week. Record your answers under the corresponding flaps.

Reflect on Learning

To complete the left-hand page, have students predict what the weather will be like each day for the upcoming week. Students should draw and label their forecast in the same format as an extended weather forecast from a local newspaper.

What's the Weather?

Type	Monday	Tuesday	Wednesday	Thursday	Friday
rainy					
sunny					
windy					
snowy					
cloudy					
Temperature					

This week's

weather was mostly …	temperature was mostly …

Weather Tools

Introduction

Discuss how weather forecasters know what the current temperature is or how much rain has fallen in the past month. Display pictures of several weather measurement tools. Explain that meteorologists use these tools to measure different types of weather. Discuss which tools measure temperature (thermometer), wind direction (weather vane), wind speed (anemometer), and rainfall (rain gauge), and how each tool works.

Note: Air pressure (barometer) and humidity (hygrometer) may be optional as these are not included in all state science standards.

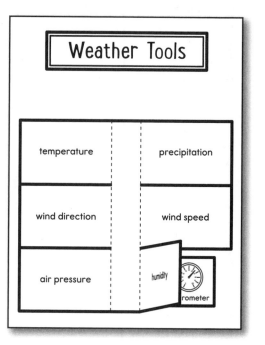

Creating the Notebook Page

Guide students through the following steps to complete the right-hand page in their notebooks.

1. Add a Table of Contents entry for the Weather Tools pages.

2. Cut out the title and glue it to the top of the page.

3. Cut out the flap book. Cut on the solid lines to create six flaps. (Cut off the bottom row of flaps if electing not to introduce hygrometer and barometer.) Apply glue to the back of the center section and attach it to the page.

4. Cut out the picture cards. Look at each one and decide what tool measures which type of weather. Glue each picture under the correct flap.

Reflect on Learning

To complete the left-hand page, have students answer the following question: *Why is it important to use measurement tools to measure weather?*

Weather Tools

temperature	precipitation
wind direction	wind speed
air pressure	humidity

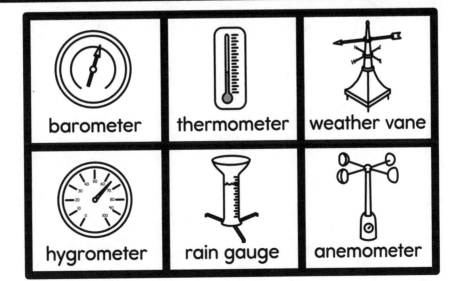

barometer · thermometer · weather vane · hygrometer · rain gauge · anemometer

How to Recycle

Introduction

Define recycling as a way to reuse items and conserve Earth's resources. Have students look around the room for things that can be recycled. Explain that most things can be recycled. Discuss the importance of using the correct recycling container when sorting recyclables. Display pictures or real recyclable objects and have students name them as plastic, paper, glass, or metal. Have students sort them into the correct groups.

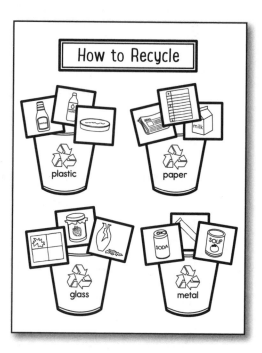

Creating the Notebook Page

Guide students through the following steps to complete the right-hand page in their notebooks.

1. Add a Table of Contents entry for the How to Recycle pages.

2. Cut out the title and glue it to the top of the page.

3. Cut out the recycling bins and glue them to the page.

4. Cut out the eight picture cards. Look at each picture and decide which recycling bin each object should be placed in. Glue each picture on or near the top of the correct recycling bin.

5. Cut out the four blank cards. On the cards, draw another object for each one of the recycling bins. Glue the cards to the corresponding bins.

Reflect on Learning

To complete the left-hand page, have students make recycling posters explaining the different types of recycling. Allow time for students to share their work.

How to Recycle

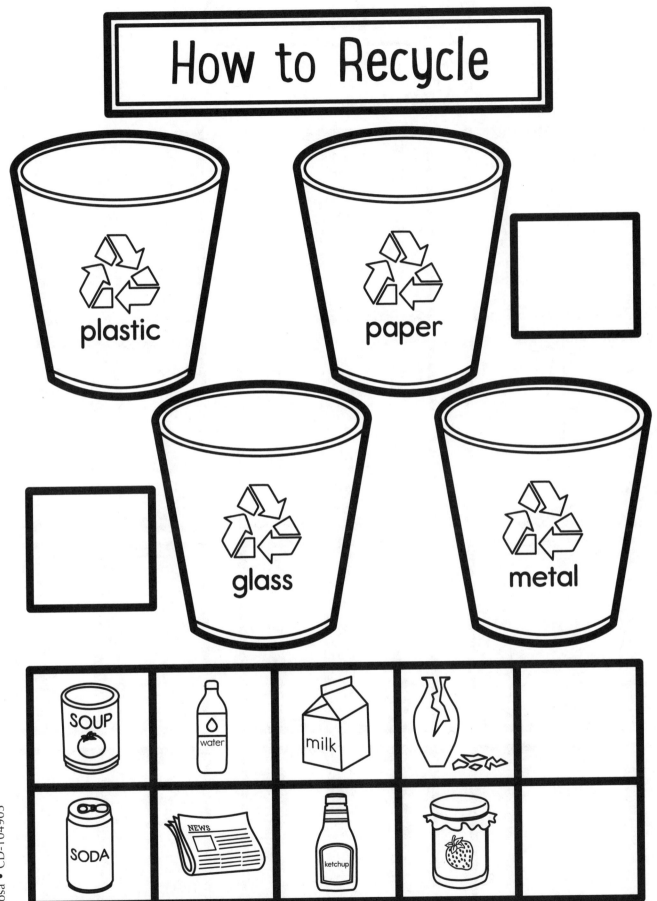

Tabs

Cut out each tab and label it. Apply glue to the back of each tab and align it on the outside edge of the page with only the label section showing beyond the edge. Then, fold each tab to seal the page inside.

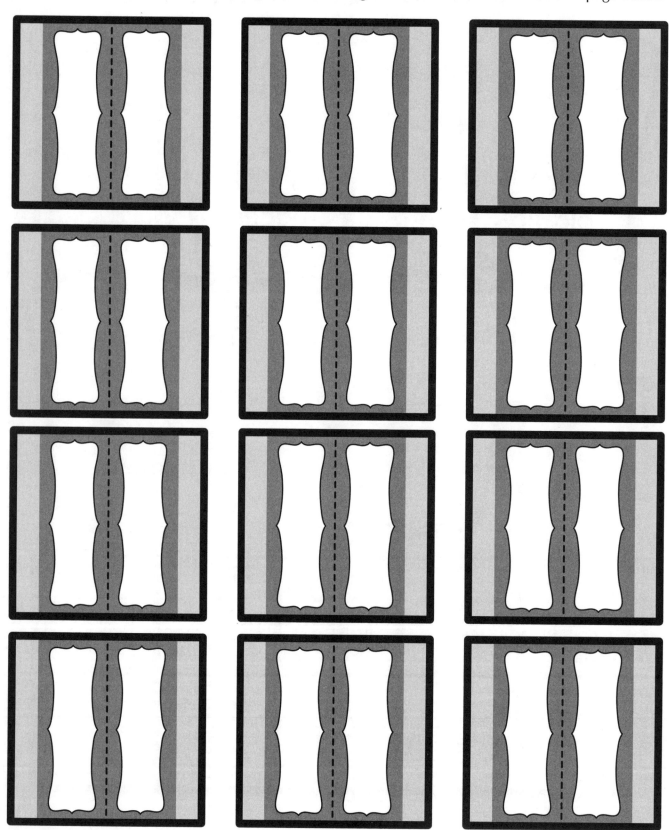

Cut out the KWL chart and cut on the solid lines to create three separate flaps. Apply glue to the back of the Topic section to attach the chart to a notebook page.

Topic:

What I

Know

What I

Wonder

What I

Learned

Library Pocket

Cut out the library pocket on the solid lines. Fold in the side tabs and apply glue to them before folding up the front of the pocket. Apply glue to the back of the pocket to attach it to a notebook page.

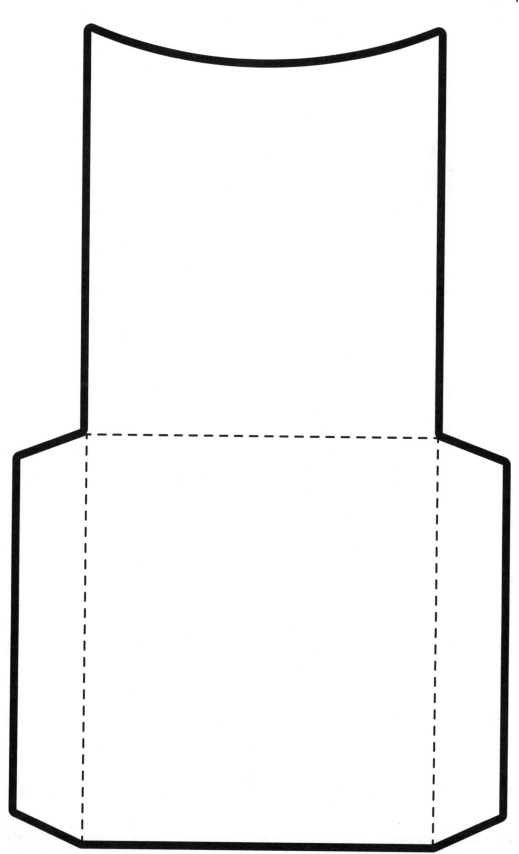

Envelope

Cut out the envelope on the solid lines. Fold in the side tabs and apply glue to them before folding up the rectangular front of the envelope. Fold down the triangular flap to close the envelope. Apply glue to the back of the envelope to attach it to a notebook page.

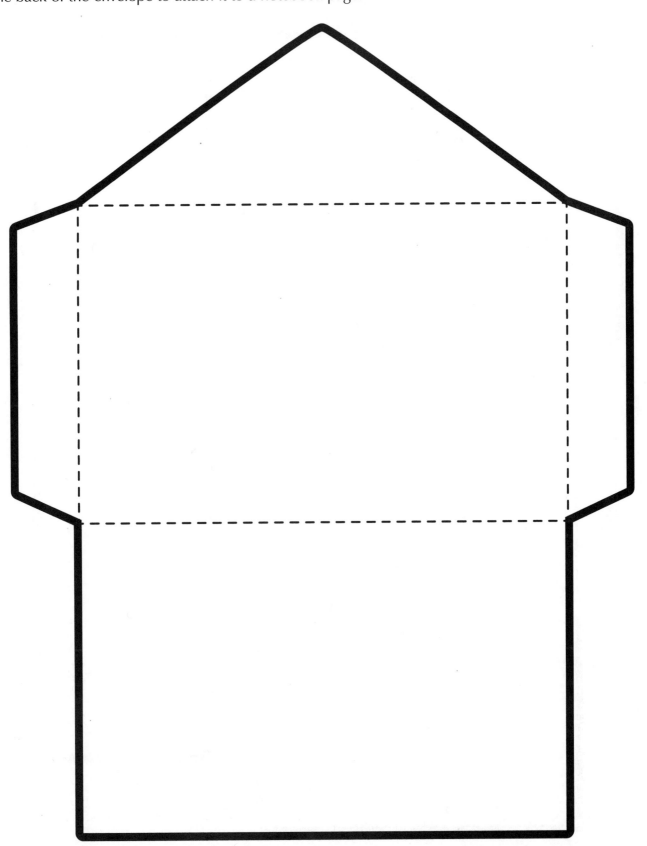

Pocket and Cards

Cut out the pocket on the solid lines. Fold over the front of the pocket. Then, apply glue to the tabs and fold them around the back of the pocket. Apply glue to the back of the pocket to attach it to a notebook page. Cut out the cards and store them in the envelope.

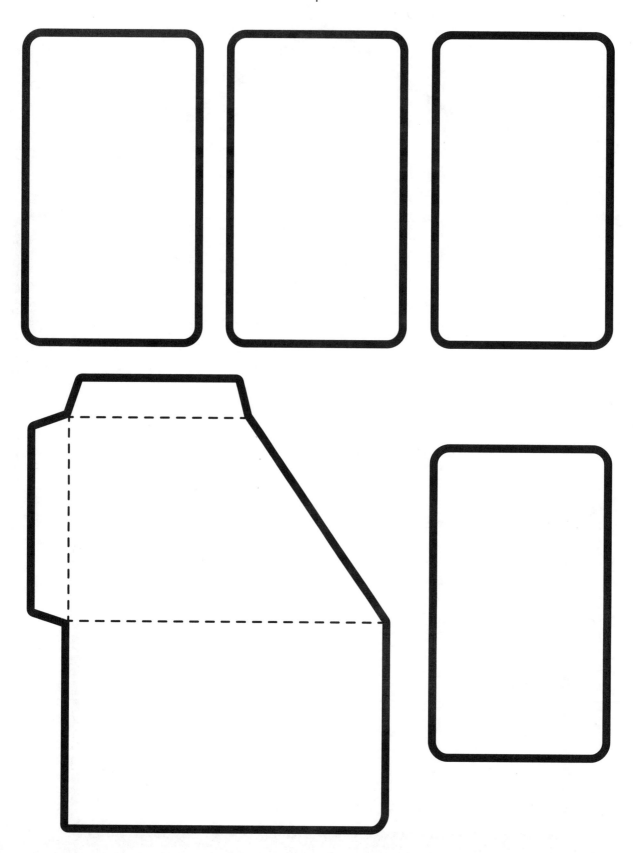

Six-Flap Shutter Fold

Cut out the shutter fold around the outside border. Then, cut on the solid lines to create six flaps. Fold the flaps toward the center. Apply glue to the back of the shutter fold to attach it to a notebook page.

If desired, this template can be modified to create a four-flap shutter fold by cutting off the bottom row. You can also create two three-flap books by cutting it in half down the center line.

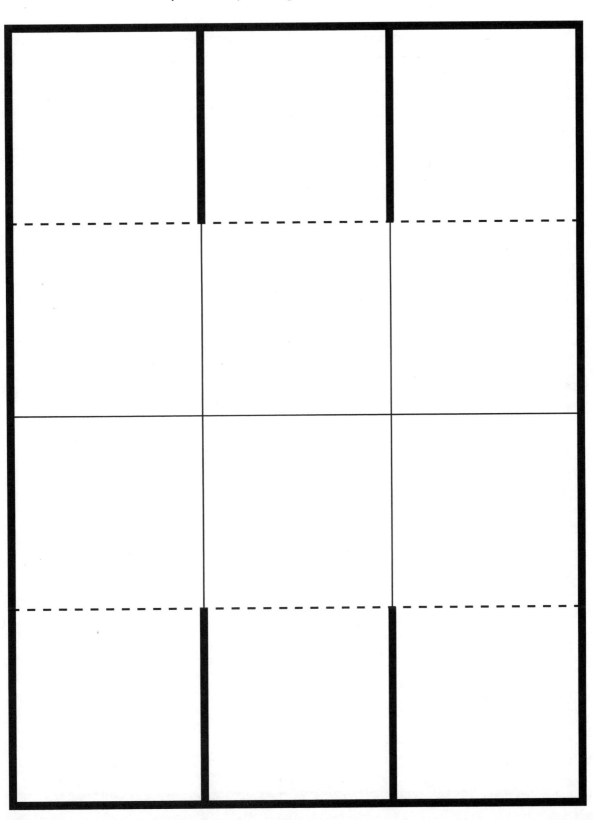

Eight-Flap Shutter Fold

Cut out the shutter fold around the outside border. Then, cut on the solid lines to create eight flaps. Fold the flaps toward the center. Apply glue to the back of the shutter fold to attach it to a notebook page.

If desired, this template can be modified to create two four-flap shutter folds by cutting off the bottom two rows. You can also create two four-flap books by cutting it in half down the center line.

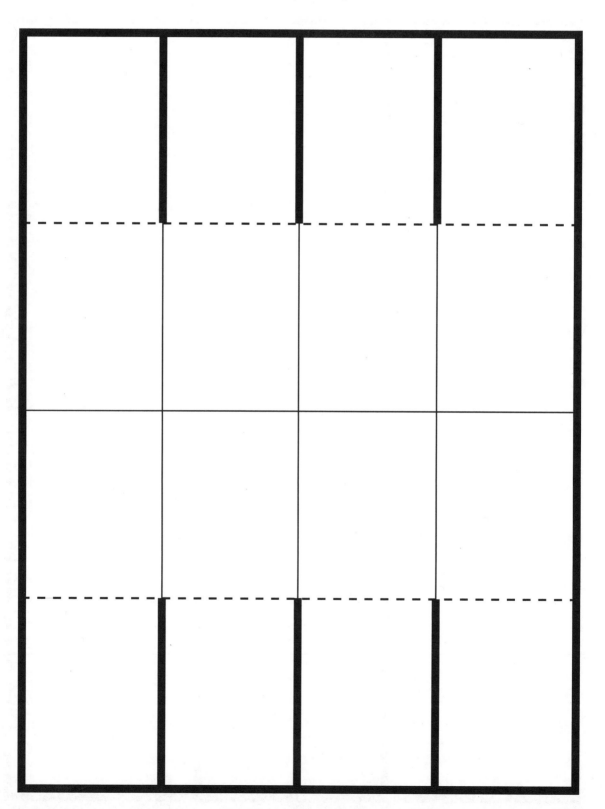

Flap Book—Eight Flaps

Cut out the flap book around the outside border. Then, cut on the solid lines to create eight flaps. Apply glue to the back of the center section to attach it to a notebook page.

If desired, this template can be modified to create a six-flap or two four-flap books by cutting off the bottom row or two. You can also create a tall four-flap book by cutting off the flaps on the left side.

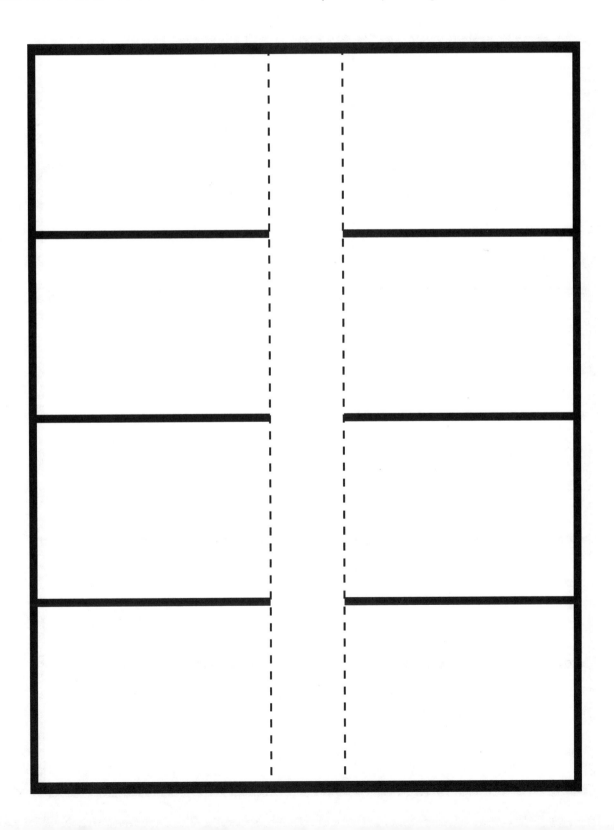

Flap Book—Twelve Flaps

Cut out the flap book around the outside border. Then, cut on the solid lines to create 12 flaps. Apply glue to the back of the center section to attach it to a notebook page.

If desired, this template can be modified to create smaller flap books by cutting off any number of rows from the bottom. You can also create a tall flap book by cutting off the flaps on the left side.

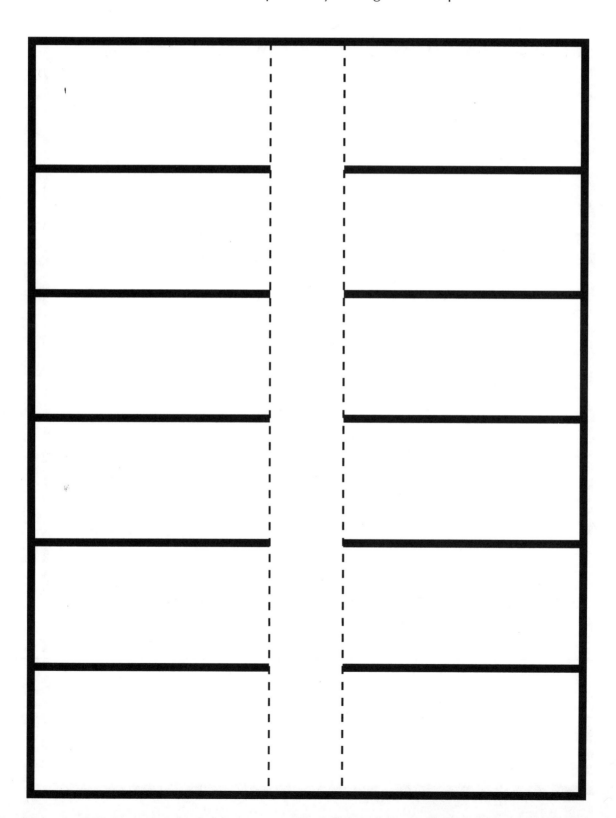

Shaped Flaps

Cut out each shaped flap. Apply glue to the back of the narrow section to attach it to a notebook page.

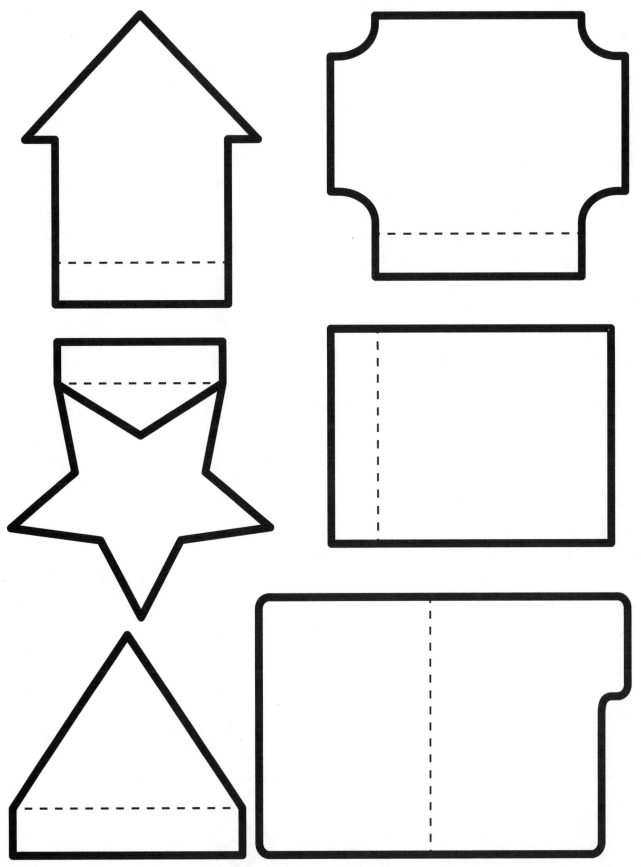

Shaped Flaps

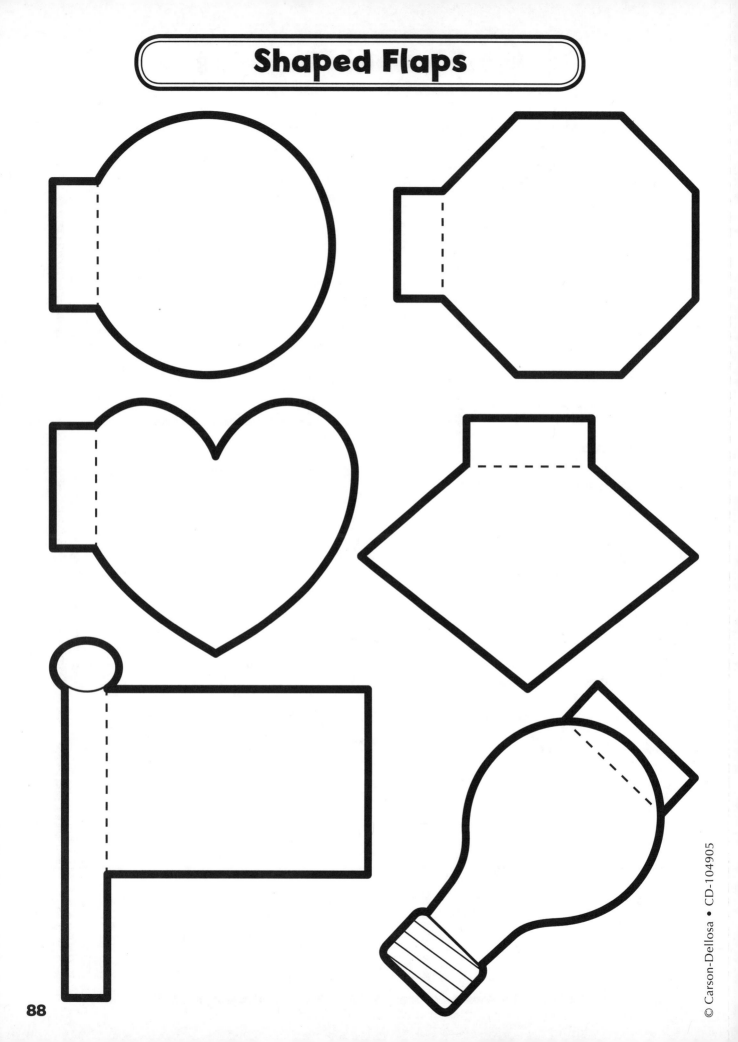

Interlocking Booklet

Cut out the booklet on the solid lines, including the short vertical lines on the top and bottom flaps. Then, fold the top and bottom flaps toward the center, interlocking them using the small vertical cuts. Apply glue to the back of the center panel to attach it to a notebook page.

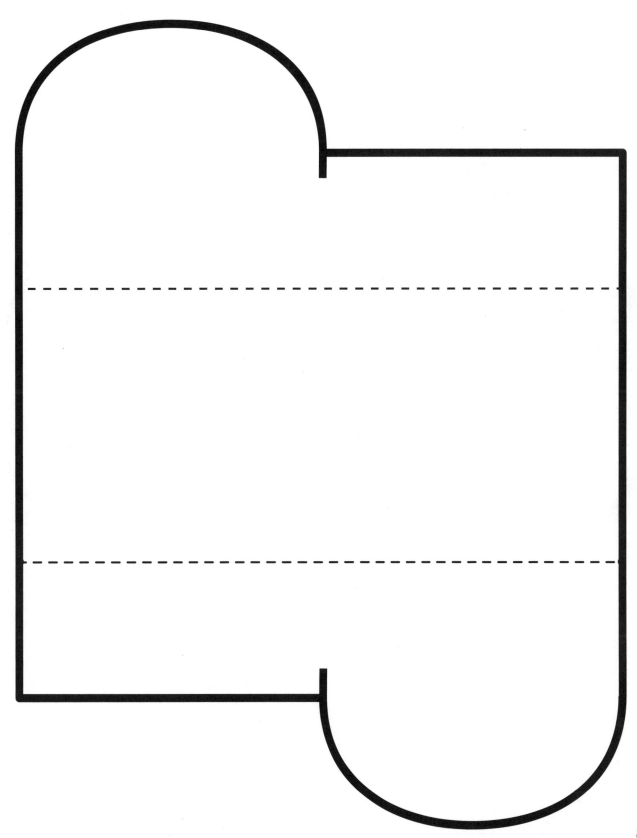

Four-Flap Petal Fold

Cut out the shape on the solid lines. Then, fold the flaps toward the center. Apply glue to the back of the center panel to attach it to a notebook page.

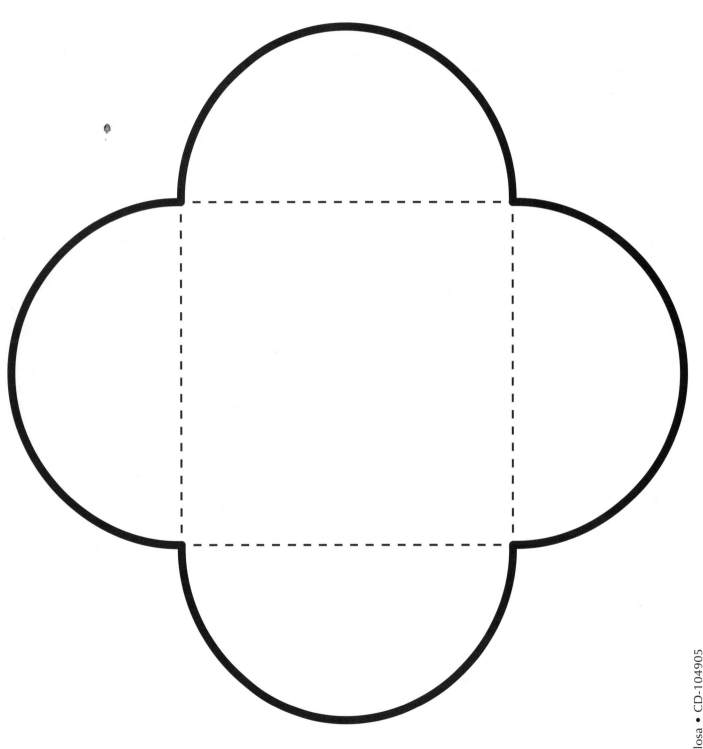

Six-Flap Petal Fold

Cut out the shape on the solid lines. Then, fold the flaps toward the center and back out. Apply glue to the back of the center panel to attach it to a notebook page.

Accordion Folds

Cut out the accordion pieces on the solid lines. Fold on the dashed lines, alternating the fold direction. Apply glue to the back of the last section to attach it to a notebook page.

You may modify the accordion books to have more or fewer pages by cutting off extra pages or by having students glue the first and last panels of two accordion books together.

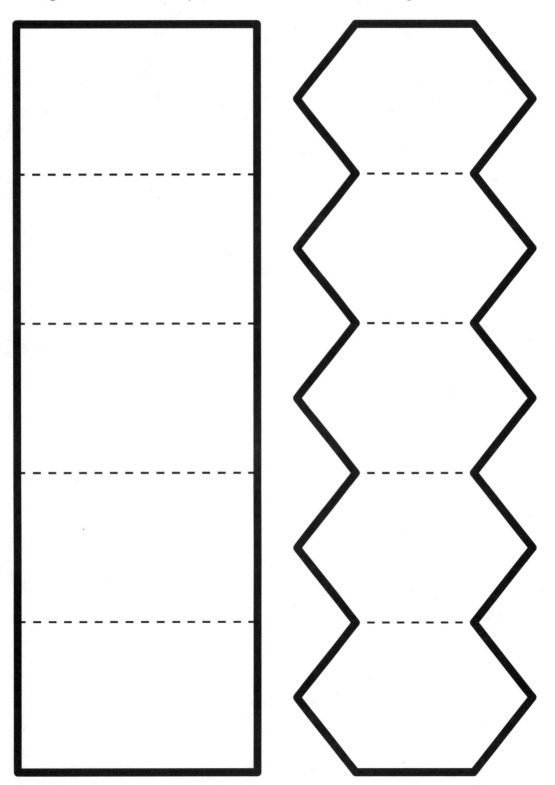

Accordion Folds

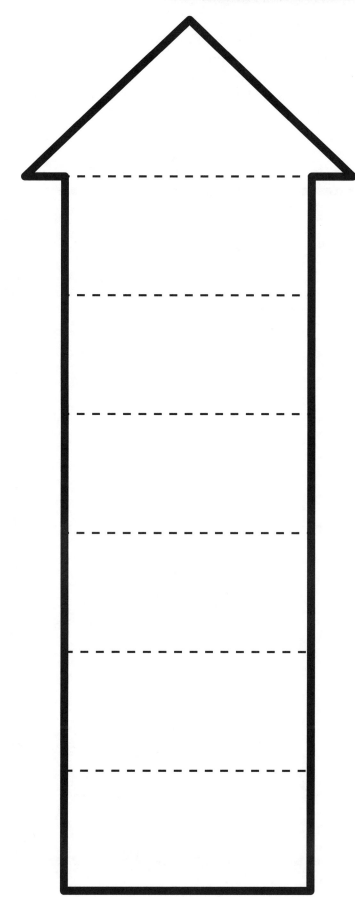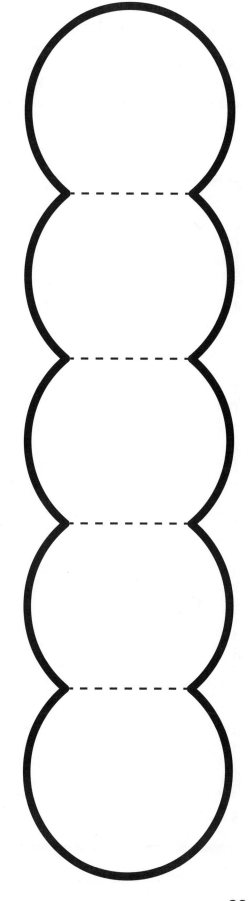

Clamshell Fold

Cut out the clamshell fold on the solid lines. Fold and unfold the piece on the three dashed lines. With the piece oriented so that the folds form an X with a horizontal line through it, pull the left and right sides together at the fold line. Then, keeping the sides touching, bring the top edge down to meet the bottom edge. You should be left with a triangular shape that unfolds into a square. Apply glue to the back of the triangle to attach the clamshell to a notebook page.

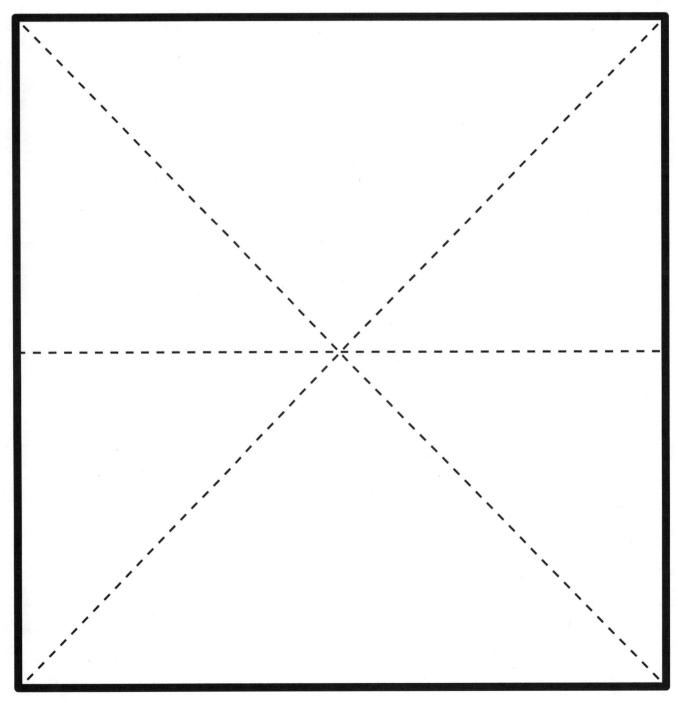

Puzzle Pieces

Cut out each puzzle along the solid lines to create a three- or four-piece puzzle. Apply glue to the back of each puzzle piece to attach it to a notebook page. Alternately, apply glue only to one edge of each piece to create flaps.

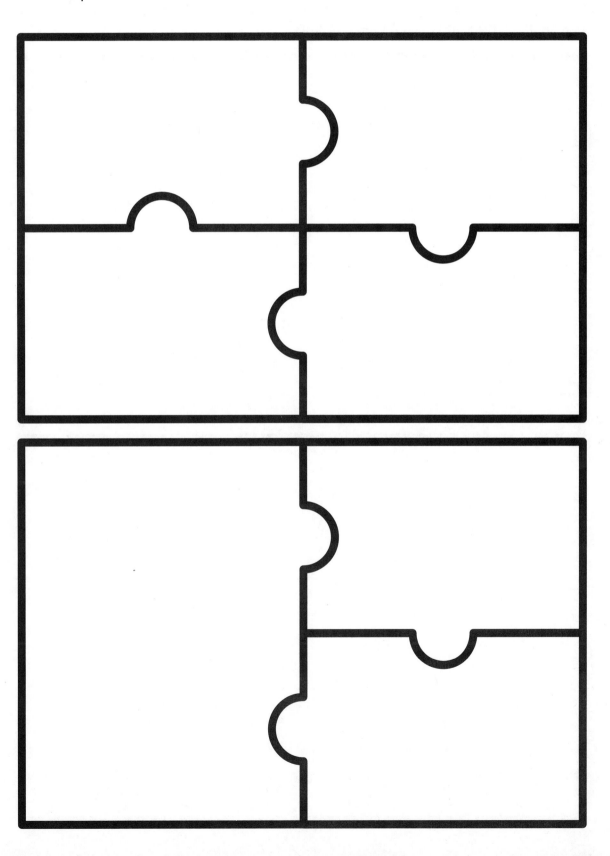

Flip Book

Cut out the two rectangular pieces on the solid lines. Fold each rectangle on the dashed lines. Fold the piece with the gray glue section so that it is inside the fold. Apply glue to the gray glue section and place the other folded rectangle on top so that the folds are nested and create a book with four cascading flaps. Make sure that the inside pages are facing up so that the edges of both pages are visible. Apply glue to the back of the book to attach it to a notebook page.

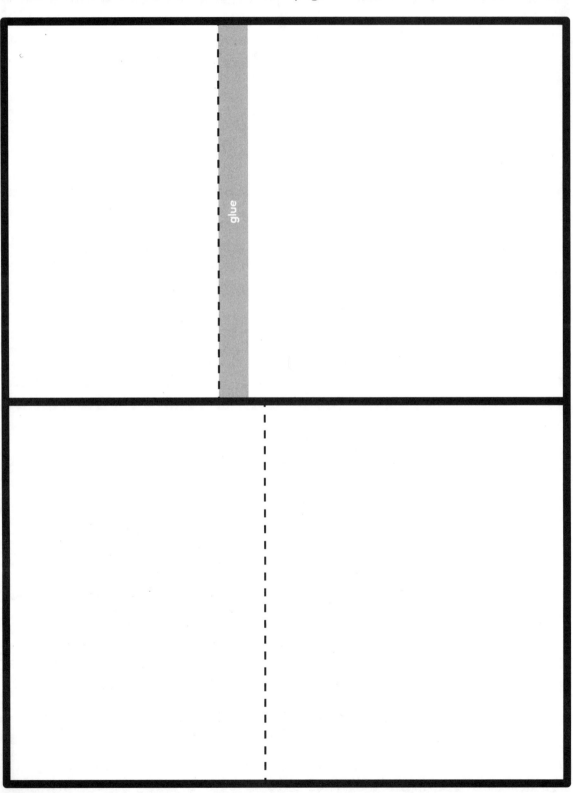

glue